HOME SKILLS

Wiring

FIX YOUR OWN LIGHTS, SWITCHES, RECEPTACLES, BOXES, CABLES & MORE

COOL SPRINGS PRESS
Home and Garden Experts™

MINNEAPOLIS, MINNESOTA

CONTENTS

Working with Wiring

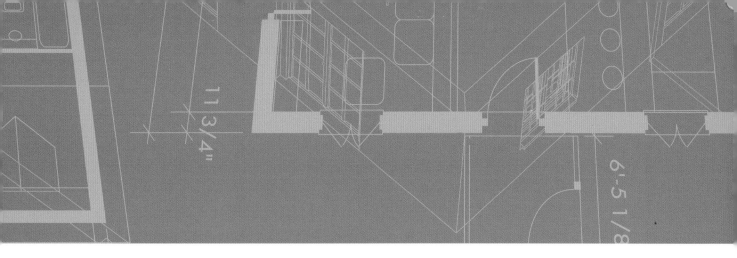

Wiring Projects

Resources

Introduction

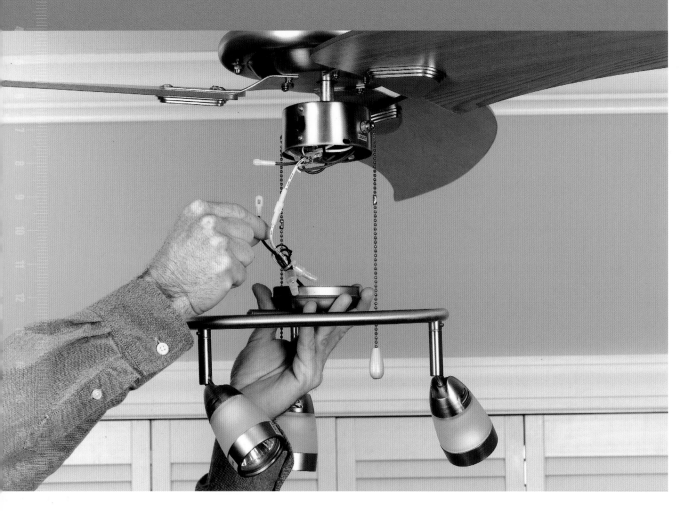

THE ELECTRICAL SYSTEM in your home may seem like a complicated, mysterious beast, ready to breathe fire or deliver shocks at any time. It is somewhat complicated, and in an older home it may actually be a dangerous beast, but the system itself is mostly straightforward. Even if you never intend to attempt a wiring project more complicated than changing out a ceiling fixture, it is important to understand how the electrical system in your home works. *HomeSkills: Wiring* explains the current standards in home wiring and explains how to test and evaluate your home's system.

Illustrations of all the most common types of electrical cables, receptacles, and switches are provided, with explanations of how they function. You will learn why it is important to update a service panel or install AFCI protection. You will learn what it means to blow a fuse or trip a circuit, how to remedy the problem, and whether something should be done as a longer-term solution.

Detailed directions for installing in either new construction or finished areas are given. Most wiring tasks do not require high levels of skill. They do, however, require a great deal of attention to the details of meeting the current codes which protect us from dangerous and costly misuse of wiring. Safety is very important when dealing with something as powerful as electricity. Hundreds of people die each year from electrocution, or from fires started by improper wiring. Make sure that your wiring project is safe and appropriate by getting a permit and having your work inspected.

WORKING WITH WIRING

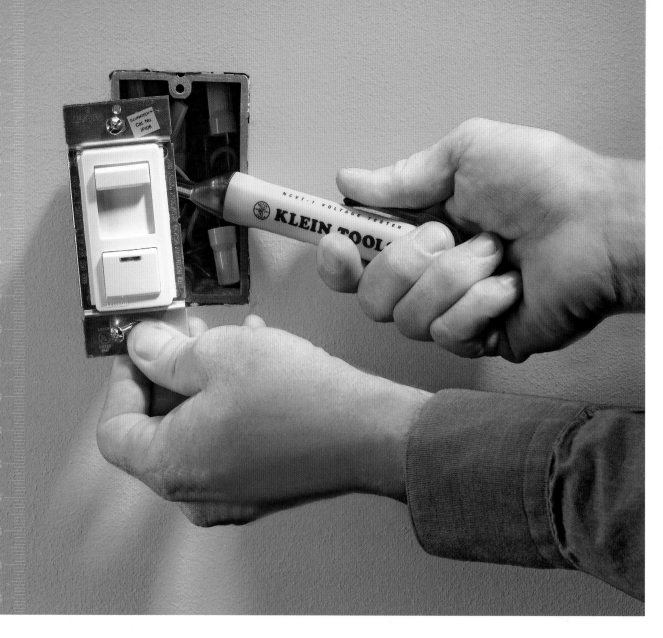

Knowing which tools are safest to use is one of the keys to successful work. Touchless circuit testers let you diagnose voltage without exposing wires.

THE ONLY WAY you can possibly manage home wiring projects safely is to understand how electricity works and how it is delivered from the street to the outlets in your home.

The most essential quality to appreciate about electricity is that the typical amounts that flow through the wires in your home can be fatal under certain conditions if you contact it directly. Sources estimate that up to 1,000 people are electrocuted accidentally in the U.S. every year. In addition, as many as 500 die in fires from electrical causes. Home wiring can be a very satisfying task for do-it-yourselfers, but if

you don't know what you're doing or are in any way uncomfortable with the idea of working around electricity, do not attempt it.

This chapter is intended to explain the fundamental principles behind the electrical circuits that run through our homes. It also includes some very basic tips for working safely with wiring, and it details the essential tools you'll need for the job. For the beginner it should be considered mandatory reading. Even if you have a good idea of electrical principles, take some time to review the material. A refresher course is always useful.

WIRING SAFETY

Safety should be the primary concern of anyone working with electricity. Although most household electrical jobs are simple and straightforward, always use caution and good judgment when working with electrical wiring or devices. Common sense can prevent accidents.

The basic rule of electrical safety is: Always turn off power to the area or device you are working on. At the main service panel, remove the fuse or shut off the circuit breaker that controls the circuit you are servicing. Then check to make sure the power is off by testing for power with a voltage tester.

Follow the safety tips shown on these pages. Never attempt an electrical project beyond your skill or confidence level. Never attempt to repair or replace your main service panel or service entrance head. These are jobs for a qualified electrician and require that the power company shut off power to your house.

Safety Tip
Always test a live circuit with the voltage tester to verify that the tester is working before you rely on it. Restore power only when the repair or replacement project is complete.

TIPS FOR WORKING WITH ELECTRICITY

Shut power OFF at the main service panel or the main fuse box before beginning any work.

Create a circuit index and affix it to the inside of the door to your main service panel. Update it as needed.

Confirm power is OFF by testing at the outlet, switch, or fixture with a voltage tester.

Use only UL-approved electrical parts or devices. These devices have been tested for safety by Underwriters Laboratories.

continued

Wear rubber-soled shoes while working on electrical projects. On damp floors, stand on a rubber mat or dry wooden boards.

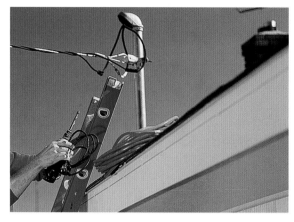

Use fiberglass or wood ladders when making routine household repairs near the service mast.

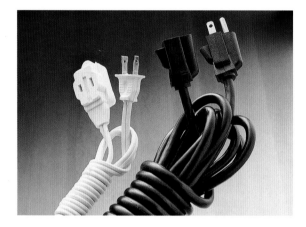

Extension cords are for temporary use only. Cords must be rated for the intended usage.

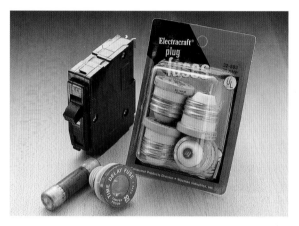

Breakers and fuses must be compatible with the panel manufacturer and match the circuit capacity.

Never alter the prongs of a plug to fit a receptacle. If possible, install a new grounded receptacle.

Do not penetrate walls or ceilings without first shutting off electrical power to the circuits that may be hidden.

HOW ELECTRICITY WORKS

A household electrical system can be compared with a home's plumbing system. Electrical current flows in wires in much the same way that water flows inside pipes. Both electricity and water enter the home, are distributed throughout the house, do their "work," and exit.

In plumbing, water first flows through the pressurized water supply system. In electricity, current first flows along hot wires. Current flowing along hot wires also is pressurized. The pressure of electrical current is called voltage.

Large supply pipes can carry a greater volume of water than small pipes. Likewise, large electrical wires carry more current than small wires. This current-carrying capacity of wires is called amperage.

Water is made available for use through the faucets, spigots, and showerheads in a home. Electricity is made available through receptacles, switches, and fixtures.

Water finally leaves the home through a drain system, which is not pressurized. Similarly, electrical current flows back through neutral wires. The current in neutral wires is not pressurized and is said to be at zero voltage.

Faucet

Water flows under pressure

Water supply pipe

Drain pipe

Water returns under no pressure

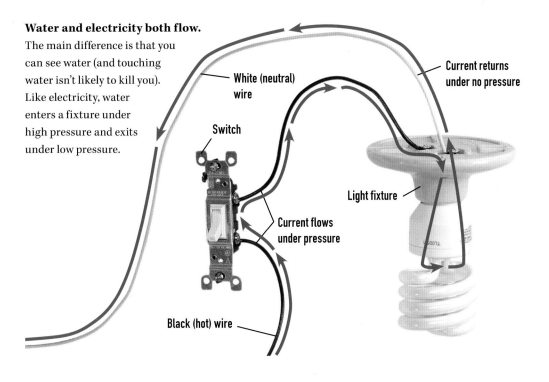

Water and electricity both flow.
The main difference is that you can see water (and touching water isn't likely to kill you). Like electricity, water enters a fixture under high pressure and exits under low pressure.

White (neutral) wire

Current returns under no pressure

Switch

Light fixture

Current flows under pressure

Black (hot) wire

Parts of the Electrical System

The service mast is the metal pole and weatherhead that create the entry point for electricity into your home. The mast is supplied with three wires carrying 240 volts and originating from the nearest transformer.

The electric meter measures the amount of electrical power consumed. It is usually attached to the side of the house, and connects to the service mast. A thin metal disc inside the meter rotates when power is used. The electric meter belongs to your local power utility company. If you suspect the meter is not functioning properly, contact the power company.

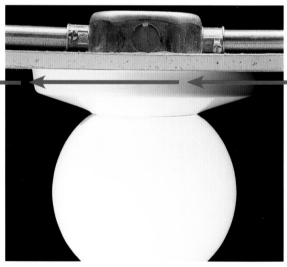

A grounding wire connects the electrical system to the earth through a metal grounding rod driven next to the house, eliminating shock hazards from equipment and metallic objects.

Light fixtures attach directly to a household electrical system. They are usually controlled with wall switches. The two common types of light fixtures are incandescent and fluorescent.

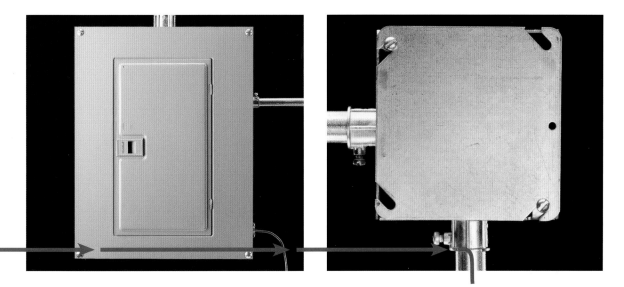

The main service panel, in the form of a fuse box or breaker box, distributes power to individual circuits. Fuses or circuit breakers protect each circuit from short circuits and overloads. Fuses and circuit breakers also are used to shut off power to individual circuits while repairs are made.

Electrical boxes enclose wire connections. According to the National Electrical Code, all wire splices or connections must be contained entirely in a covered plastic or metal electrical box.

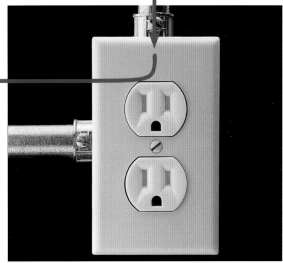

Switches control electrical current passing through hot circuit wires. Switches can be wired to control light fixtures, ceiling fans, appliances, and receptacles.

Receptacles, sometimes called outlets, provide plug-in access to electrical power. A 120-volt, 15-amp receptacle with a grounding hole is the most typical receptacle in wiring systems installed after 1965. Most receptacles have two plug-in locations and are called duplex receptacles.

Glossary of Electrical Terms

Ampere (or amp): Refers to the rate at which electrical power flows to a light, tool, or appliance.

Armored cable: Two or more wires that are grouped together and protected by a flexible metal covering.

Box: A device used to contain wiring connections.

BX: See armored cable (Bx is the older term).

Cable: Two or more wires that are grouped together and protected by a covering or sheath.

Circuit: A continuous loop of electrical current flowing along wires or cables.

Circuit breaker: A safety device that interrupts an electrical circuit in the event of an overload or short circuit.

Conductor: Any material that allows electrical current to flow through it. Copper wire is an especially good conductor.

Conduit: A metal or plastic pipe used to protect wires.

Continuity: An uninterrupted electrical pathway through a circuit or electrical fixture.

Current: The movement of electrons along a conductor.

Duplex receptacle: A receptacle that provides connections for two plugs.

Feed wire: A conductor that carries 120-volt current uninterrupted from the service panel.

Fuse: A safety device, usually found in older homes, that interrupts electrical circuits during an overload or short circuit.

Greenfield: Materials used in flexible metal conduit. See armored cable.

Grounded wire: See neutral wire.

Grounding wire: A wire used in an electrical circuit to conduct current to the earth in the event of a short circuit. The grounding wire often is a bare copper wire.

Hot wire: Any wire that carries voltage. In an electrical circuit, the hot wire usually is covered with black or red insulation.

Insulator: Any material, such as plastic or rubber, that resists the flow of electrical current. Insulating materials protect wires and cables.

Junction box: See box.

Meter: A device used to measure the amount of electrical power being used.

Neutral wire: A wire that returns current at zero voltage to the source of electrical power. Usually covered with white or light gray insulation. Also called the grounded wire.

Non-metallic sheathed cable: NM cable consists of two or more insulated conductors and, in most cases, a bare ground wire housed in a durable PVC casing.

Outlet: See receptacle.

Overload: A demand for more current than the circuit wires or electrical device was designed to carry. Usually causes a fuse to blow or a circuit breaker to trip.

Pigtail: A short wire used to connect two or more circuit wires to a single screw terminal.

Polarized receptacle: A receptacle designed to keep hot current flowing along black or red wires, and neutral current flowing along white or gray wires.

Power: The result of hot current flowing for a period of time. Use of power makes heat, motion, or light.

Receptacle: A device that provides plug-in access to electrical power.

Romex: A brand name of plastic-sheathed electrical cable that is commonly used for indoor wiring. Commonly known as NM cable.

Screw terminal: A place where a wire connects to a receptacle, switch, or fixture.

Service panel: A metal box usually near the site where electrical power enters the house. In the service panel, electrical current is split into individual circuits. The service panel has circuit breakers or fuses to protect each circuit.

Short circuit: An accidental and improper contact between two current-carrying wires, or between a current-carrying wire and a grounding conductor.

Switch: A device that controls electrical current passing through hot circuit wires. Used to turn lights and appliances on and off.

UL: An abbreviation for Underwriters Laboratories, an organization that tests electrical devices and manufactured products for safety.

Voltage (or volts): A measurement of electricity in terms of pressure.

Wattage (or watt): A measurement of electrical power in terms of total energy consumed. Watts can be calculated by multiplying the voltage times the amps.

Wire connector: A device used to connect two or more wires together. Also called a wire nut.

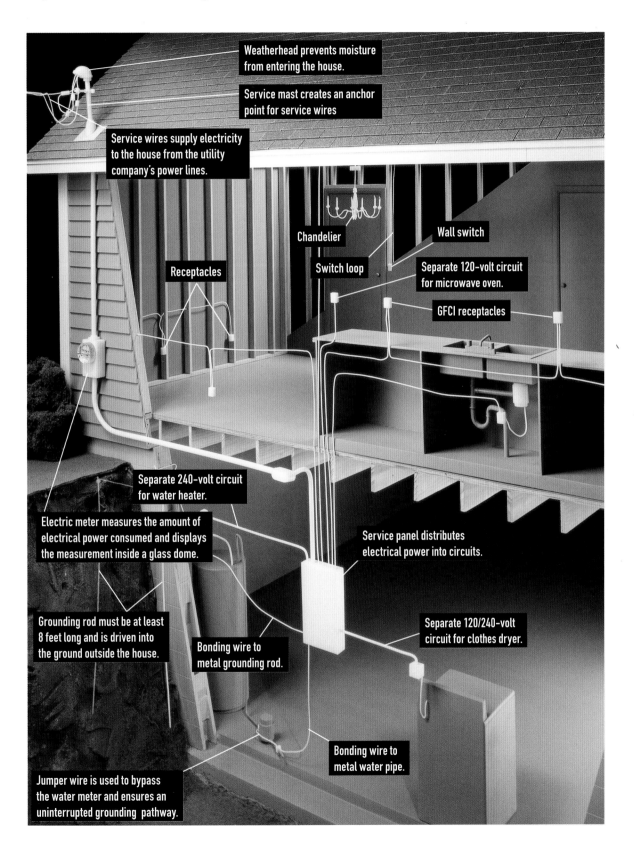

Weatherhead prevents moisture from entering the house.

Service mast creates an anchor point for service wires

Service wires supply electricity to the house from the utility company's power lines.

Chandelier

Wall switch

Receptacles

Switch loop

Separate 120-volt circuit for microwave oven.

GFCI receptacles

Separate 240-volt circuit for water heater.

Electric meter measures the amount of electrical power consumed and displays the measurement inside a glass dome.

Service panel distributes electrical power into circuits.

Grounding rod must be at least 8 feet long and is driven into the ground outside the house.

Bonding wire to metal grounding rod.

Separate 120/240-volt circuit for clothes dryer.

Bonding wire to metal water pipe.

Jumper wire is used to bypass the water meter and ensures an uninterrupted grounding pathway.

UNDERSTANDING ELECTRICAL CIRCUITS

An electrical circuit is a continuous loop. Household circuits carry power from the main service panel, throughout the house, and back to the main service panel. Several switches, receptacles, light fixtures, or appliances may be connected to a single circuit.

Current enters a circuit loop on hot wires and returns along neutral wires. These wires are color coded for easy identification. Hot wires are black or red, and neutral wires are white or light gray. For safety, most circuits include a bare copper or green insulated grounding wire. The grounding wire conducts current in the event of a ground fault, and helps reduce the chance of severe electrical shock. The service panel also has a grounding wire connected to a metal water pipe and metal grounding rod buried underground.

If a circuit carries too much power, it can overload. A fuse or a circuit breaker protects each circuit in case of overloads.

Current returns to the service panel along a neutral circuit wire. Current then becomes part of a main circuit and leaves the house on a large neutral service wire that returns it to the utility pole transformer.

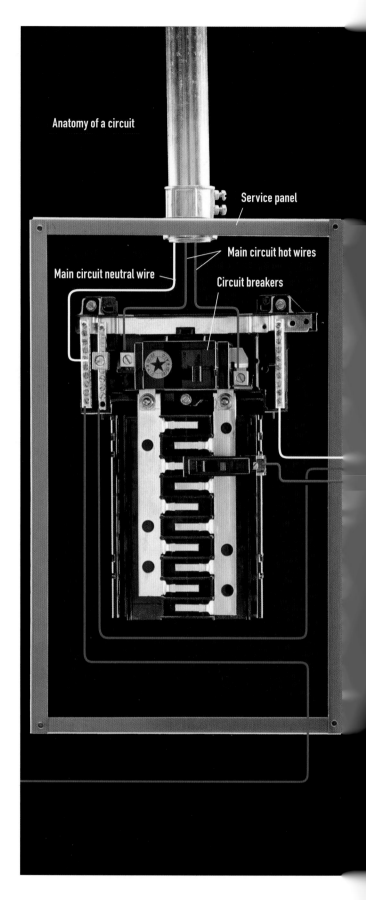

Anatomy of a circuit

Service panel

Main circuit hot wires

Main circuit neutral wire

Circuit breakers

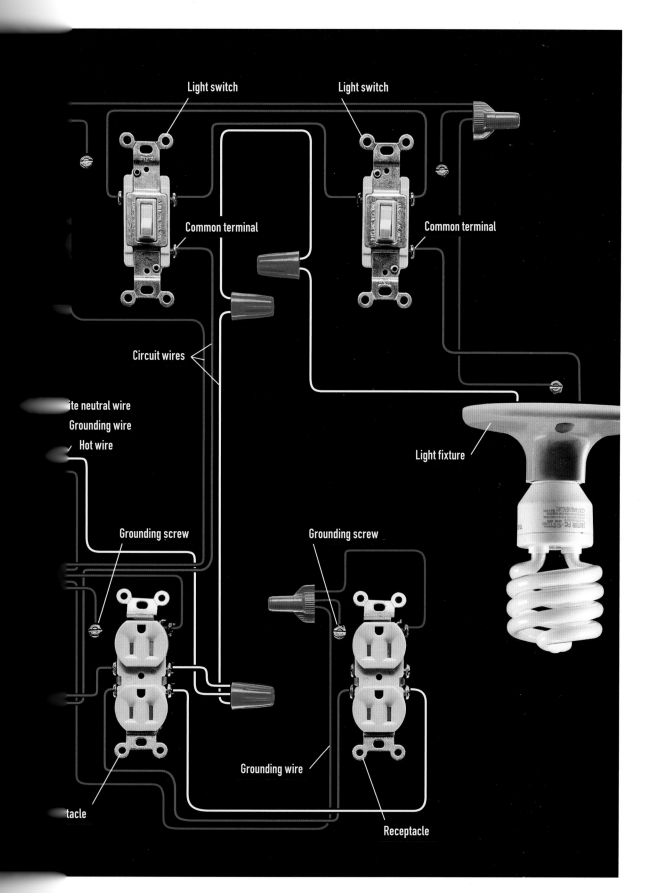

Light switch

Light switch

Common terminal

Common terminal

Circuit wires

ite neutral wire

Grounding wire

Hot wire

Light fixture

Grounding screw

Grounding screw

Grounding wire

tacle

Receptacle

GROUNDING & POLARIZATION

Electricity always seeks to return to its source and complete a continuous circuit. In a household wiring system, this return path is provided by white neutral wires that return current to the main service panel. From the service panel, current returns along a neutral service wire to a power pole transformer.

A grounding wire provides an additional return path for electrical current. The grounding wire is a safety feature. It is designed to conduct electricity if current seeks to return to the service panel along a path other than the neutral wire, a condition known as a ground fault.

A ground fault is a potentially dangerous situation. If an electrical box, tool, or appliance becomes short-circuited and is touched by a person, the electrical current may attempt to return to its source by passing through that person's body.

However, electrical current prefers the path of least resistance. A grounding wire provides a safe, easy path for current to follow back to its utility transformer. If a person touches an electrical box, tool, or appliance that has a properly installed grounding wire, any chance of receiving a severe electrical shock is greatly reduced.

In addition, household wiring systems are required to be connected directly to the earth. This helps to ensure that all equipment and metallic objects are held at Earth's potential (zero volts) to eliminate shock hazards. A short circuit can also occur when a hot and a neutral conductor come in contact. When your electrical system is functioning properly, the fuses or circuit breaker will de-energize the circuit to clear the fault.

Grounding of the home electrical system is accomplished by wiring the household electrical system to a metal cold water pipe and metal grounding rods that are buried in the earth.

After 1920, most American homes included receptacles that accepted polarized plugs. The two-slot polarized plug and receptacle was designed to keep hot current flowing along black or red wires, and neutral current flowing along white or gray wires.

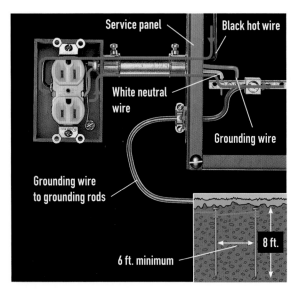

Normal current flow: Current enters the electrical box along a black hot wire, then returns to the service panel along a white neutral wire. Any excess current passes into the earth via a grounding wire attached to grounding rods or a metal water pipe.

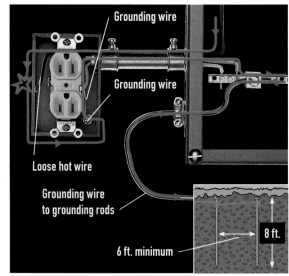

Short circuit: Current is detoured by a loose wire in contact with the metal box. The grounding wire picks it up and channels it safely back to the main service panel. There, it returns to its source along a neutral service cable or enters the earth via the grounding system.

Armored cable and metal conduit, widely installed in homes during the 1940s, provided a true grounding path. When connected to metal junction boxes, it provided a metal pathway back to the service panel.

Modern cable includes a green insulated or bare copper wire that serves as the grounding path. This grounding wire is connected to all three-slot receptacles and metal boxes to provide a continuous pathway for any ground faulted current. By plugging a three-prong plug into a grounded three-slot receptacle, people are protected from ground faults that occur in appliances, tools or other electric devices.

Use a receptacle adapter to plug three-prong plugs into two-slot receptacles, but use it only if the receptacle connects to a grounding wire or grounded electrical box. Adapters have short grounding wires or wire loops that attach to the receptacle's coverplate mounting screw. The mounting screw connects the adapter to the grounded metal electrical box.

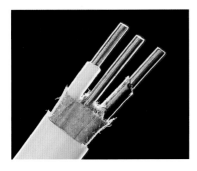

Modern NM (nonmetallic) cable, found in most wiring systems installed after 1965, contains a bare copper wire that provides grounding for receptacle and switch boxes.

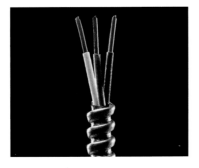

Armored cable is sold pre-installed in a flexible metal housing. BX, Greenfield, and MC are three common types. Metal-clad cable Type MC is shown here. It contains a green insulated ground wire along with black and white conductors.

Polarized receptacles have a long slot and a short slot. Used with a polarized plug, the polarized receptacle keeps electrical current directed for safety.

Three-slot receptacles are required by code for new homes. They are usually connected to a standard two-wire cable with ground.

Receptacle adapter allows three-prong plugs to be inserted into two-slot receptacles. The adapter can be used only with grounded receptacles, and the grounding loop or wire of the adapter must be attached to the coverplate mounting screw of the receptacle. Use of these adapters is generally discouraged.

Double-insulated tools have non-conductive plastic bodies to prevent shocks caused by short circuits. Because of these features, double-insulated tools can be used safely with ungrounded receptacles.

HOME WIRING TOOLS

To complete the wiring projects shown in this book, you need a few specialty electrical tools as well as a collection of basic hand tools. As with any tool purchase, invest in good-quality products when you buy tools for electrical work. Keep your tools clean, and sharpen or replace any cutting tools that have dull edges.

The materials used for electrical wiring have changed dramatically in the last 20 years, making it much easier for homeowners to do their own electrical work.

> **Tip**
> Electrical tape is never actually used to splice or repair electrical wires. If you see electrical tape used on any wiring in your home without a wire cap, the problem needs to be corrected immediately by re-making the connection with a cap.

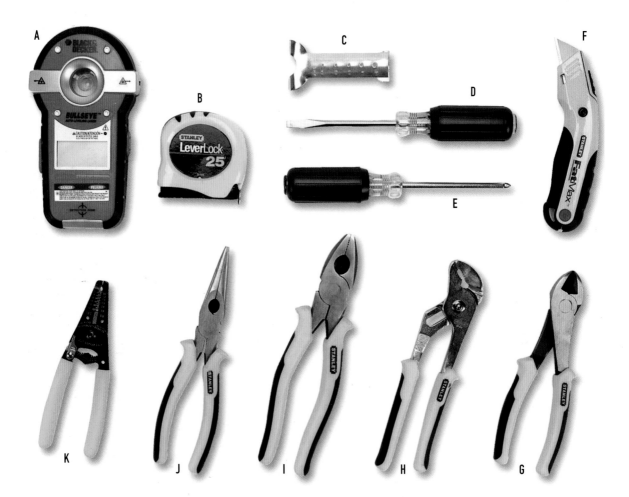

Hand tools you'll need for home wiring projects include: Stud finder/laser level (A) for locating framing members and aligning electrical boxes; Tape measure (B); Cable ripper (C) for scoring NM sheathing; Standard (D) and Phillips (E) screwdrivers; Utility knife (F); Side cutters (G) for cutting wires; Channel-type pliers (H) for general gripping and crimping; Linesman pliers (I) combine side cutter and gripping jaws; Needlenose pliers (J); Wire strippers (K) for removing insulation from conductors.

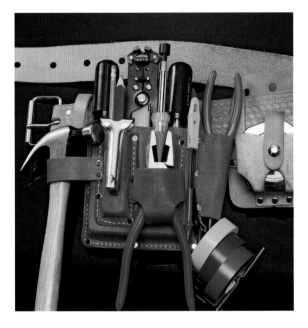

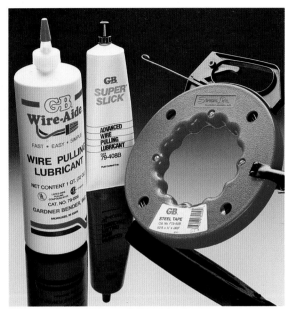

Use a tool belt to keep frequently used tools within easy reach. Electrical tapes in a variety of colors are used for marking wires and for attaching cables to a fish tape.

A fish tape is useful for installing cables in finished wall cavities and for pulling wires through conduit. Products designed for lubrication reduce friction and make it easier to pull cables and wires.

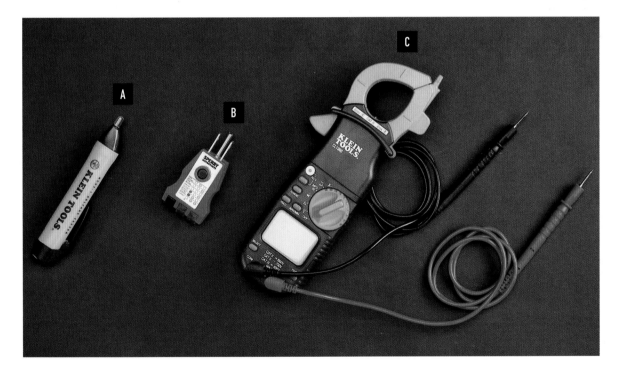

Diagnostic tools for home wiring use include: Touchless circuit tester (A) to safely check wires for current and confirm that circuits are dead; Plug-in tester (B) to check receptacles for correct polarity, grounding, and circuit protection; Multimeter (C) to measure AC/DC voltage, AC/DC current, resistance, capacitance, frequency, and duty cycle (model shown is an auto-ranging digital multimeter with clamp-on jaws that measure through sheathing and wire insulation).

WIRE & CABLE

Wires are made of copper, aluminum, or aluminum covered with a thin layer of copper. Solid copper wires are the best conductors of electricity and are the most widely used. Aluminum and copper-covered aluminum wires require special installation techniques.

A group of two or more wires enclosed in a metal, rubber, or plastic sheath is called a cable (photo, opposite page). The sheath protects the wires from damage. Metal conduit also protects wires, but it is not considered a cable.

Individual wires are covered with rubber or plastic vinyl insulation. An exception is a bare copper grounding wire, which does not need an insulation cover. The insulation is color coded (chart, left) to identify the wire as a hot wire, a neutral wire, or a grounding wire.

In most wiring systems installed after 1965, the wires and cables are insulated with plastic vinyl. This type of insulation is very durable and can last as long as the house itself.

Before 1965, wires and cables were insulated with rubber. Rubber insulation has a life expectancy of about 25 years. Old insulation that is cracked or damaged can be reinforced temporarily by wrapping the wire with plastic electrical tape. However, old wiring with damaged insulation should be inspected by a qualified electrician to make sure it is safe.

Wires must be large enough for the amperage rating of the circuit (chart, right). A wire that is too small can become dangerously hot. Wire sizes are categorized according to the American Wire Gauge (AWG) system. To check the size of a wire, use the wire stripper openings of a combination tool as a guide.

Wire Color Chart

Wire Color		Function
	White	Neutral wire carrying current at zero voltage.
	Black	Hot wire carrying current at full voltage.
	Red	Hot wire carrying current at full voltage.
	White, black markings	Hot wire carrying current at full voltage.
	Green	Serves as a grounding pathway.
	Bare copper	Serves as a grounding pathway.

Individual wires are color-coded to identify their function. In some circuit installations, the white wire serves as a hot wire that carries voltage. If so, this white wire may be labeled with black tape or paint to identify it as a hot wire.

Wire Size Chart

Wire Gauge		Wire Capacity and Use
	#6	60 amps, 240 volts; central air conditioner, electric furnace.
	#8	40 amps, 240 volts; electric range, central air conditioner.
	#10	30 amps, 240 volts; window air conditioner, clothes dryer.
	#12	20 amps, 120 volts; light fixtures, receptacles, microwave oven.
	#14	15 amps, 120 volts; light fixtures, receptacles.
	#16	Light-duty extension cords.
	#18 to 22	Thermostats, doorbells, security systems.

Wire sizes (shown actual size) are categorized by the American Wire Gauge system. The larger the wire size, the smaller the AWG number.

Knob and tube wiring, so called because of the shape of its porcelain insulating brackets, was common before 1940. Wires are covered with a layer of rubberized cloth fabric, but have no additional protection.

Metal-clad (MC) armored cable has been around since the 1920s. Early versions had no grounding function, but existed solely to protect the wires that were threaded into it. Later armored cable products either had ground wire twisted in with the flexible metal cover or relied on the metal cover itself for connecting to ground. Modern MC contains an insulated ground wire along with the conductors.

Metal conduit was installed during the middle of the 20th century as a way to protect hot and neutral conductors. The conduit itself often was employed for connecting to ground. Modern conduit (both metal and PVC) should be filled with insulated THHN conductors, including an insulated ground wire.

Early NM (nonmetallic) cable was used from 1930 until 1965. It features a rubberized fabric sheathing that protects individual wires. NM cable greatly simplified installations because separate wires no longer had to be pulled by hand through a conduit or armored cable. Early NM cable had no grounding wire.

NM (nonmetallic) cable was developed around 1930. The first version had rubberized sheathing that degraded rapidly and had no ground wire. Modern versions with a hard PVC shell came onto the market in the 1960s. Sheathing is now color-coded by gauge (the yellow seen here is 12 AWG).

UF (underground feeder) cable has wires embedded in a solid-core plastic vinyl sheathing and includes a bare copper grounding wire. It is designed for installations in damp conditions, such as buried circuits.

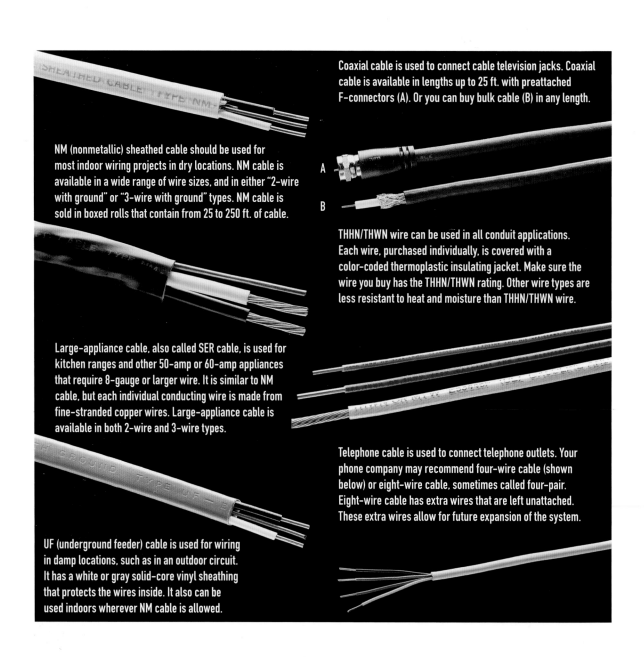

Coaxial cable is used to connect cable television jacks. Coaxial cable is available in lengths up to 25 ft. with preattached F-connectors (A). Or you can buy bulk cable (B) in any length.

NM (nonmetallic) sheathed cable should be used for most indoor wiring projects in dry locations. NM cable is available in a wide range of wire sizes, and in either "2-wire with ground" or "3-wire with ground" types. NM cable is sold in boxed rolls that contain from 25 to 250 ft. of cable.

A

B

THHN/THWN wire can be used in all conduit applications. Each wire, purchased individually, is covered with a color-coded thermoplastic insulating jacket. Make sure the wire you buy has the THHN/THWN rating. Other wire types are less resistant to heat and moisture than THHN/THWN wire.

Large-appliance cable, also called SER cable, is used for kitchen ranges and other 50-amp or 60-amp appliances that require 8-gauge or larger wire. It is similar to NM cable, but each individual conducting wire is made from fine-stranded copper wires. Large-appliance cable is available in both 2-wire and 3-wire types.

Telephone cable is used to connect telephone outlets. Your phone company may recommend four-wire cable (shown below) or eight-wire cable, sometimes called four-pair. Eight-wire cable has extra wires that are left unattached. These extra wires allow for future expansion of the system.

UF (underground feeder) cable is used for wiring in damp locations, such as in an outdoor circuit. It has a white or gray solid-core vinyl sheathing that protects the wires inside. It also can be used indoors wherever NM cable is allowed.

Tips for Working with Wire

Wire Gauge		Ampacity	Maximum Wattage Load
	14-gauge	15 amps	1440 watts (120 volts)
	12-gauge	20 amps	1920 watts (120 volts) 3840 watts (240 volts)
	10-gauge	30 amps	2880 watts (120 volts) 5760 watts (240 volts)
	8-gauge	40 amps	7680 watts (240 volts)
	6-gauge	50 amps	9600 watts (240 volts)

Wire "ampacity" is a measurement of how much current a wire can carry safely. Ampacity varies according to the size of the wires, as shown at left. When installing a new circuit, choose wire with an ampacity rating matching the circuit size. For dedicated appliance circuits, check the wattage rating of the appliance and make sure it does not exceed the maximum wattage load of the circuit.

Reading NM (Nonmetallic) Cable

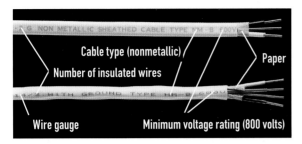

Cable type (nonmetallic)

Number of insulated wires

Paper

Wire gauge

Minimum voltage rating (800 volts)

Reading Unsheathed, Individual Wire

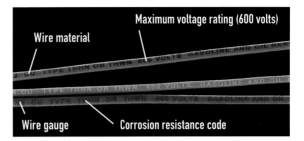

Wire material

Maximum voltage rating (600 volts)

Wire gauge

Corrosion resistance code

NM (nonmetallic) cable is labeled with the number of insulated wires it contains. The bare grounding wire is not counted. For example, a cable marked 14/2 G (or 14/2 WITH GROUND) contains two insulated 14-gauge wires, plus a bare copper grounding wire. Cable marked 14/3 WITH GROUND has three 14-gauge wires plus a grounding wire. NM cable also is stamped with a maximum voltage rating, as determined by Underwriters Laboratories (UL).

Unsheathed, individual wires are used for conduit and raceway installations. Wire insulation is coded with letters to indicate resistance to moisture, heat, and gas or oil. Code requires certain letter combinations for certain applications. T indicates thermoplastic insulation. H stands for heat resistance and two Hs indicate high resistance (up to 194° F). W denotes wire suitable for wet locations. Wire coded with an N is impervious to damage from oil or gas.

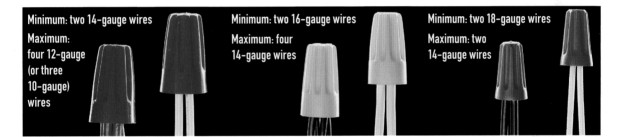

Minimum: two 14-gauge wires
Maximum: four 12-gauge (or three 10-gauge) wires

Minimum: two 16-gauge wires
Maximum: four 14-gauge wires

Minimum: two 18-gauge wires
Maximum: two 14-gauge wires

Use wire connectors rated for the wires you are connecting. Wire connectors are color-coded by size, but the coding scheme varies according to manufacturer. The wire connectors shown above come from one major manufacturer. To ensure safe connections, each connector is rated for both minimum and maximum wire capacity. These connectors can be used to connect both conducting wires and grounding wires. Green wire connectors are used only for grounding wires.

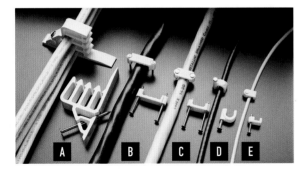

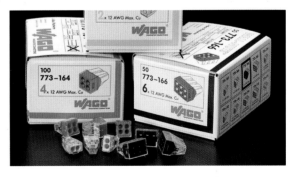

Use plastic cable staples to fasten cables. Choose staples sized to match the cables. Stack-It® staples (A) hold up to four 2-wire cables; ¾" staples (B) for 12/2, 12/3, and all 10-gauge cables; ½" staples (C) for 14/2, 14/3, or 12/2 cables; coaxial staples (D) for anchoring television cables; bell wire staples (E) for attaching telephone cables.

Push-in connectors are a relatively new product for joining wires. Instead of twisting the bare wire ends together, you strip off about ¾" of insulation and insert them into a hole in the connector. The connectors come with two to four holes sized for various gauge wires. These connectors are perfect for inexperienced DIYers because they do not pull apart like a sloppy twisted connection can.

1   Measure and mark the cable 8 to 10" from end. Slide the cable ripper onto the cable, and squeeze tool firmly to force cutting point through plastic sheathing.

2   Grip the cable tightly with one hand, and pull the cable ripper toward the end of the cable to cut open the plastic sheathing.

3   Peel back the plastic sheathing and the paper wrapping from the individual wires.

4   Cut away the excess plastic sheathing and paper wrapping, using the cutting jaws of a combination tool.

5   Cut individual wires as needed using the cutting jaws of the combination tool. Leave a minimum of 6" of wire running past the edge of the box.

6   Strip insulation for each wire, using the stripper openings. Choose the opening that matches the gauge of the wire, and take care not to nick or scratch the ends of the wires.

Tip
It's a good idea to practice stripping wire and cable before you strip wire you have installed.

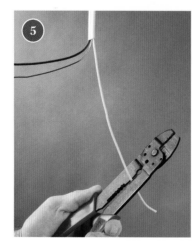

Cutting point

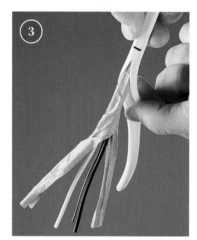

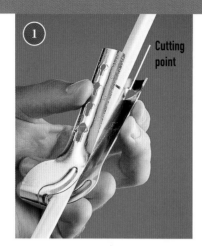

Cutting jaws

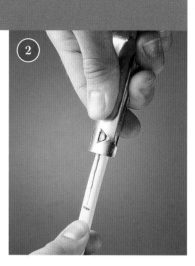

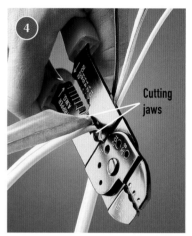

Wire stripper openings

CONNECTING WIRES TO SCREW TERMINALS

1   Strip about ¾" of insulation from each wire using a combination tool. Choose the stripper opening that matches the gauge of the wire, then clamp the wire in the tool. Pull the wire firmly to remove plastic insulation.

2   Form a C-shaped loop in the end of each wire using a needlenose pliers or the hole of the correct gauge in a pair of wire strippers. The wire should have no scratches or nicks.

3   Hook each wire around the screw terminal so it forms a clockwise loop. Tighten screw firmly. Insulation should just touch head of screw. Never place the ends of two wires under a single screw terminal. Instead, use a pigtail wire (page 27).

CONNECTING WIRES WITH PUSH-INS

1   Mark the amount of insulation to be stripped from each wire using the strip gauge on the back of the switch or receptacle. Strip the wires using a combination tool (step 1, above). Never use push-in fittings with aluminum wiring.

2   Insert the bare copper wires firmly into the push-in fittings on the back of the switch or receptacle. When inserted, wires should have no bare copper exposed. Note: Although push-in fittings are convenient, most experts believe screw terminal connections (above) are more dependable.

3   Remove a wire from a push-in fitting by inserting a small nail or screwdriver in the release opening next to the wire. Wire will pull out easily.

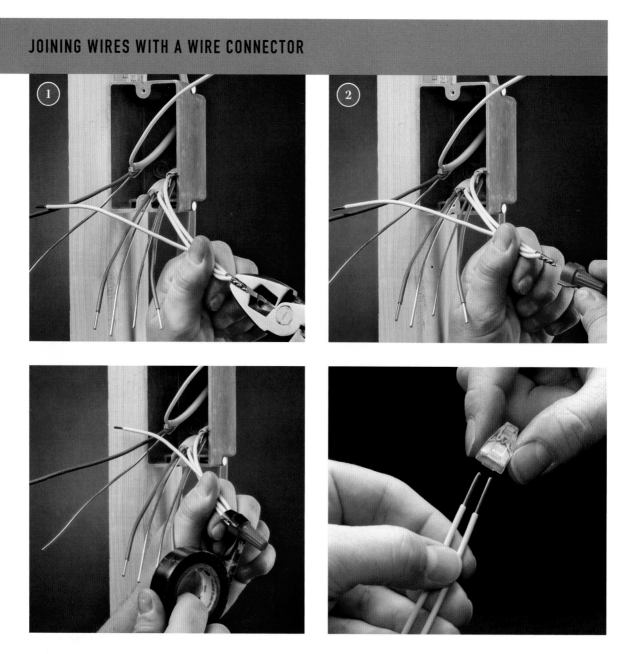

1   Ensure power is off and test for power. Grasp the wires to be joined in the jaws of a pair of linesman's pliers. The ends of the wires should be flush and they should be parallel and touching. Rotate the pliers clockwise two or three turns to twist the wire ends together.

2   Twist a wire connector over the ends of the wires. Make sure the connector is the right size (see page 23). Hand-twist the connector as far onto the wires as you can. There should be no bare wire exposed beneath the collar of the connector.

    Option: Reinforce the joint by wrapping it with electrician's tape. By code, you cannot bind the wire joint with tape only, but it can be used as insurance. Few professional electricians use tape for purposes other than tagging wires for identification.

    Option: Strip ¾" of insulation off the ends of the wires to be joined, and insert each wire into a push-in connector. Gently tug on each wire to make sure it is secure.

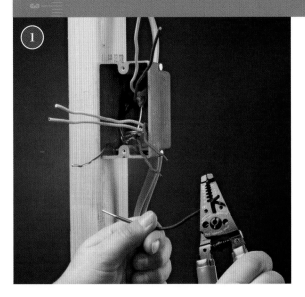

1 Cut a 6" length from a piece of insulated wire the same gauge and color as the wires it will be joining. Strip ¾" of insulation from each end of the insulated wire.

2 Join one end of the pigtail to the wires that will share the connection using a wire nut (see previous page).

3 Connect the pigtail to the appropriate terminal on the receptacle or switch. Fold the wires neatly and press the fitting into the box.

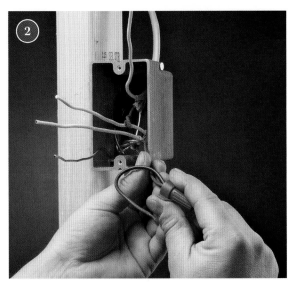

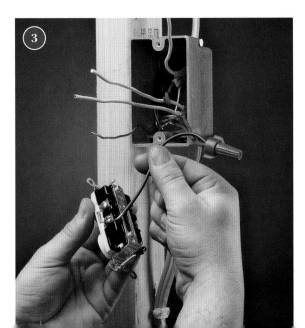

Alternative:

If you are pigtailing to a grounding screw or grounding clip in a metal box, you may find it easier to attach one end of the wire to the grounding screw before you attach the other end to the other wires.

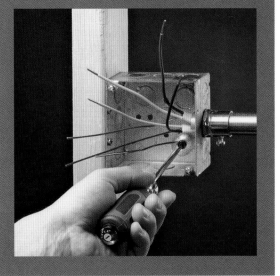

Tip

Pigtailing is done mainly to avoid connecting multiple wires to one terminal, which is a code violation.

NM CABLE

NM cable is used for all indoor wiring projects except those requiring conduit. Cut and install the cable after all electrical boxes have been mounted. Refer to your wiring plan to make sure each length of cable is correct for the circuit size and configuration.

Cable runs are difficult to measure exactly, so leave plenty of extra wire when cutting each length. Cable splices inside walls are not allowed by code. When inserting cables into a circuit breaker panel, make sure the power is shut off.

After all cables are installed and all the ground wires spliced, call your electrical inspector to arrange for the rough-in inspection. Do not install wallboard or attach light fixtures and other devices until this inspection is done.

Tools & Materials

Drill	NM cable
Bits	Cable clamps
Tape measure	Cable staples
Cable ripper	Masking tape
Combination tool	Electrical tape
Screwdrivers	Grounding pigtails
Needlenose pliers	Wire connectors
Hammer	Eye and ear protection
Fish tape	

Pulling cables through studs is easier if you drill smooth, straight holes at the same height. Prevent kinks by straightening the cable before pulling it through the studs. Use plastic grommets to protect cables on steel studs (inset).

Framing Member	Maximum Hole Size	Maximum Notch Size
2 × 4 loadbearing stud	1⁷⁄₁₆" diameter	⅞" deep
2 × 4 non-loadbearing stud	2½" diameter	1⁷⁄₁₆" deep
2 × 6 loadbearing stud	2¼" diameter	1⅜" deep
2 × 6 non-loadbearing stud	3⁵⁄₁₆" diameter	2³⁄₁₆" deep
2 × 6 joists	1½" diameter	⅞" deep
2 × 8 joists	2⅜" diameter	1¼" deep
2 × 10 joists	3¹⁄₁₆" diameter	1½" deep
2 × 12 joists	3¾" diameter	1⅞" deep

This framing member chart shows the maximum sizes for holes and notches that can be cut into studs and joists when running cables. When boring holes, there must be at least 1¼" of wood between the edge of a stud and the hole, and at least 2" between the edge of a joist and the hole. Joists can be notched only in the end ⅓ of the overall span; never in the middle ⅓ of the joist. If 1¼" clearance cannot possibly be maintained, you may be able to satisfy code by installing a metal nail plate over the point of penetration in the stud.

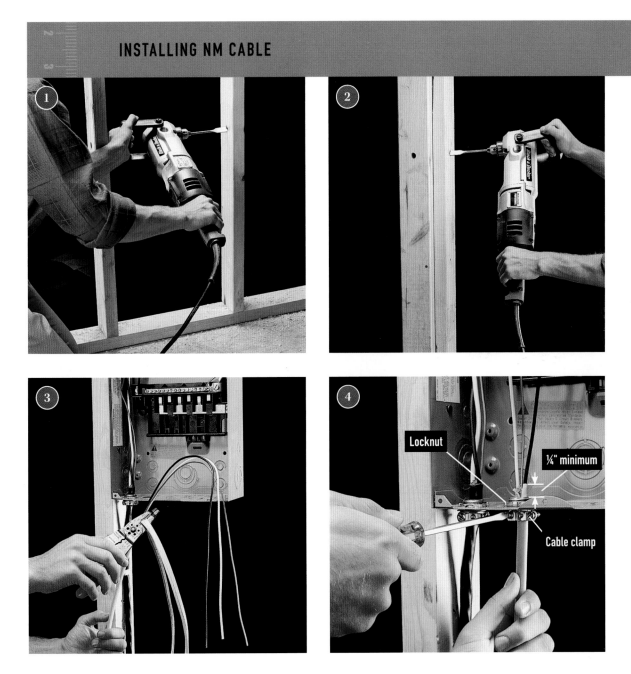

1 Drill ⅝" holes in framing members for the cable runs. This is done easily with a right-angle drill, available at rental centers. Holes should be set back at least 1¼" from the front face of the framing members.

2 Where cables will turn corners (step 6, page 30), drill intersecting holes in adjoining faces of studs. Measure and cut all cables, allowing 2 ft. extra at ends entering the breaker panel and 1 ft. for ends entering the electrical box.

3 Shut off power to circuit breaker panel. Use a cable ripper to strip cable, leaving at least ¼" of sheathing to enter the circuit breaker panel. Clip away the excess sheathing.

4 Open a knockout in the circuit breaker panel using a hammer and screwdriver. Insert a cable clamp into the knockout, and secure it with a locknut. Insert the cable through the clamp so that at least ¼" of sheathing extends inside the circuit breaker panel. Tighten the mounting screws on the clamp so the cable is gripped securely but not so tightly that the sheathing is crushed.

continued

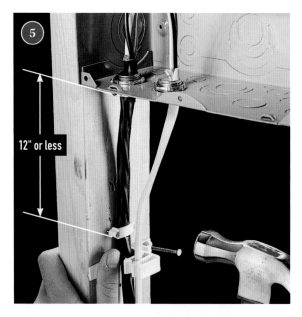

12" or less

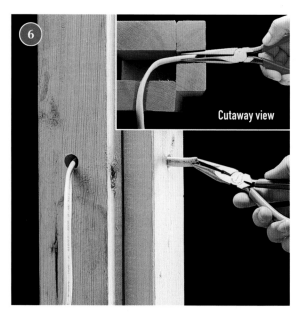

Cutaway view

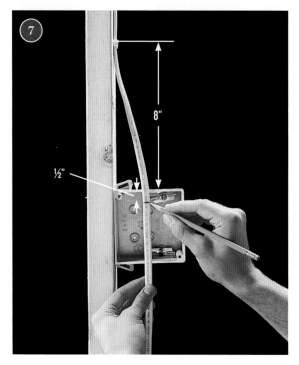

8"

½"

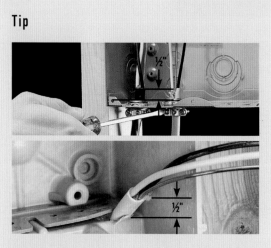

½"

½"

Tip

Different types of boxes have different clamping devices. Make sure cable sheathing extends ½" past the edge of the clamp to ensure that the cable is secure and that the wire won't be damaged by the edges of the clamp.

5   Anchor the cable to the center of a framing member within 12" of the circuit breaker panel using a cable staple. Stack-It® staples work well where two or more cables must be anchored to the same side of a stud. Run the cable to the first electrical box. Where the cable runs along the sides of framing members, anchor it with cable staples no more than 4 ft. 6 in. apart.

6   At corners, form a slight L-shaped bend in the end of the cable and insert it into one hole. Retrieve the cable through the other hole using needlenose pliers (inset).

7   Staple the cable to a framing member 8" from the box. Hold the cable taut against the front of the box, and mark a point on the sheathing ½" past the box edge. Remove sheathing from the marked line to the end using a cable ripper, and clip away excess sheathing with a combination tool. Insert the cable through the knockout in the box.

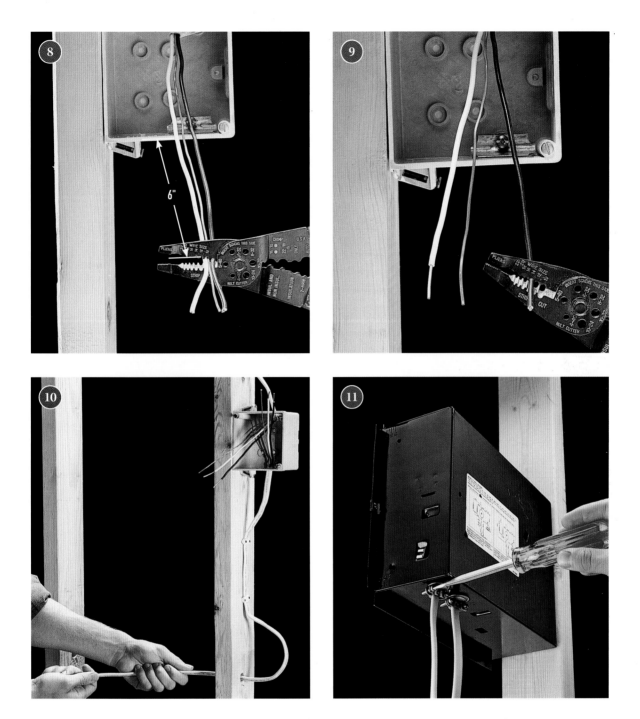

8   As each cable is installed in a box, clip back each wire so that at least 6" of workable wire extends past the front edge of the box.

9   Strip ¾" of insulation from each circuit wire in the box using a combination tool. Take care not to nick the copper.

10 Continue the circuit by running cable between each pair of electrical boxes, leaving an extra 1 ft. of cable at each end.

11 At metal boxes and recessed fixtures, open knockouts, and attach cables with cable clamps. From inside fixture, strip away all but ¼" of sheathing. Clip back wires so there is 8" of workable length, then strip ¾" of insulation from each wire.

continued

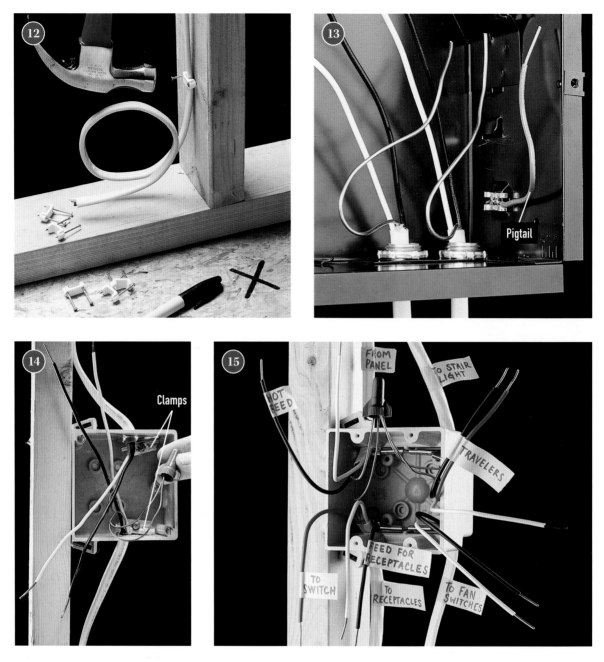

12 For a surface-mounted fixture like a baseboard heater or fluorescent light fixture, staple the cable to a stud near the fixture location, leaving plenty of excess cable. Mark the floor so the cable will be easy to find after the walls are finished.

13 At each recessed fixture and metal electrical box, connect one end of a grounding pigtail to the metal frame using a grounding clip attached to the frame (shown above) or a green grounding screw.

14 At each electrical box and recessed fixture, join grounding wires together with a wire connector. If the box has internal clamps, tighten the clamps over the cables.

15 Label the cables entering each box to indicate their destinations. In boxes with complex wiring configurations, also tag the individual wires to make final hookups easier. After all cables are installed, your rough-in work is ready to be reviewed by the electrical inspector.

Run Cable Inside Finished Walls

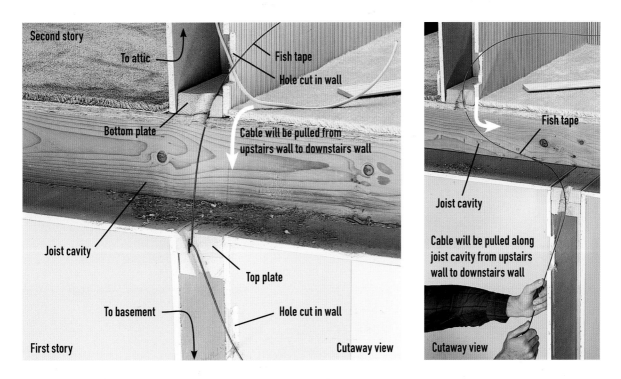

If there is no access space above and below a wall, cut openings in the finished walls to run a cable. This often occurs in two-story homes when a cable is extended from an upstairs wall to a downstairs wall. Cut small openings in the wall near the top and bottom plates, then drill an angled 1" hole through each plate. Extend a fish tape into the joist cavity between the walls and use it to pull the cable from one wall to the next. If the walls line up one over the other (left), you can retrieve the fish tape using a piece of stiff wire. If walls do not line up (right), use a second fish tape. After running the cable, repair the holes in the walls with patching plaster or wallboard scraps and taping compound.

If you don't have a fish tape, use a length of sturdy string and a lead weight or heavy washer. Drop the line into the stud cavity from above, then use a piece of stiff wire to hook the line from below.

Use a flexible drill bit, also called a bell-hanger's bit, to bore holes through framing in finished walls.

1   From the unfinished space below the finished wall, look for a reference point, like a soil stack, plumbing pipes, or electrical cables, that indicates the location of the wall above. Choose a location for the new cable that does not interfere with existing utilities. Drill a 1" hole up into the stud cavity.

2   From the unfinished space above the finished wall, find the top of the stud cavity by measuring from the same fixed reference point used in step 1. Drill a 1" hole down through the top plate and into the stud cavity using a drill bit extender.

3   Extend a fish tape down through the top plate, twisting the tape until it reaches the bottom of the stud cavity. From the unfinished space below the wall, use a piece of stiff wire with a hook on one end to retrieve the fish tape through the drilled hole in the bottom plate.

4   Trim back 2" of sheathing from the end of the NM cable, then insert the wires through the loop at the tip of the fish tape.

5   Bend the wires against the cable, then use electrical tape to bind them tightly. Apply cable-pulling lubricant to the taped end of the fish tape.

6   From above the finished wall, pull steadily on the fish tape to draw the cable up through the stud cavity. This job will be easier if you have a helper feed the cable from below as you pull.

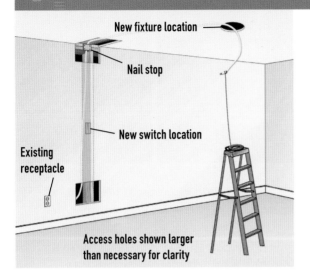

New fixture location

Nail stop

New switch location

Existing receptacle

Access holes shown larger than necessary for clarity

If you don't have access to a ceiling from above, you can run cable for a new ceiling fixture from an existing receptacle in the room up the wall and into the ceiling without disturbing much of the ceiling. To begin, run cable from the receptacle to the stud channel that aligns with the ceiling joists on which you want to install a fixture. Be sure to plan a location for the new switch. Remove short strips of drywall from the wall and ceiling. Make a notch in the center of the top plates, and protect the notch with metal nail stops. Use a fish tape to pull the new cable up through the wall cavity and the notch in top plates. Next, use the fish tape to pull the cable through the ceiling to the fixture hole. After having your work inspected, replace the drywall and install the fixture and switch.

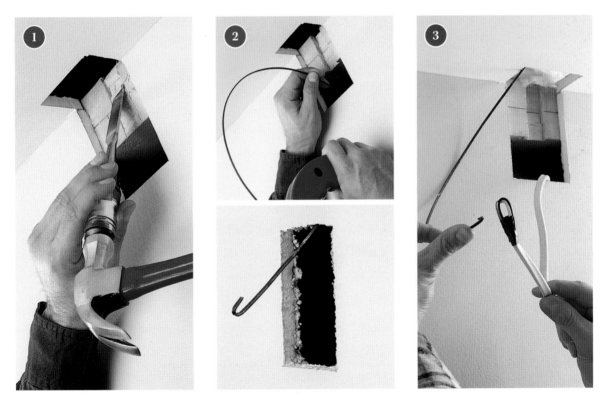

1. Plan a route for running cable between electrical boxes (see illustration above). Remove drywall on the wall and ceiling surface. Where cable must cross framing members, cut a small access opening in the wall and ceiling surface; then cut a notch into the framing with a wood chisel.

2. Fish a cable from the existing receptacle location up to the notch at the top of the wall. Protect the notch with a metal nail stop.

3. Fish the cable through the ceiling to the location of the new ceiling fixture.

CONDUIT

Electrical wiring that runs in exposed locations must be protected by rigid tubing called conduit. For example, conduit is used for wiring that runs across masonry walls in a basement laundry and for exposed outdoor wiring. THHN/THWN wire normally is installed inside conduit, although UF or NM cable can also be installed in conduit.

There are several types of conduit available, so check with your electrical inspector to find out which type meets code requirements in your area. Conduit installed outdoors must be rated for exterior use. Metal conduit should be used only with metal boxes, never with plastic boxes.

At one time, conduit could only be fitted by using elaborate bending techniques and special tools. Now, however, a variety of shaped fittings are available to let a homeowner join conduit easily.

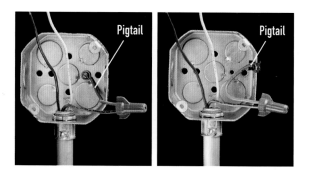

Electrical Grounding in Metal Conduit: Install a green insulated grounding wire for any circuit that runs through metal conduit. Although code allows the metal conduit to serve as the grounding conductor, most electricians install a green insulated wire as a more dependable means of grounding the system. The grounding wires must be connected to metal boxes with a pigtail and grounding screw (left) or grounding clip (right).

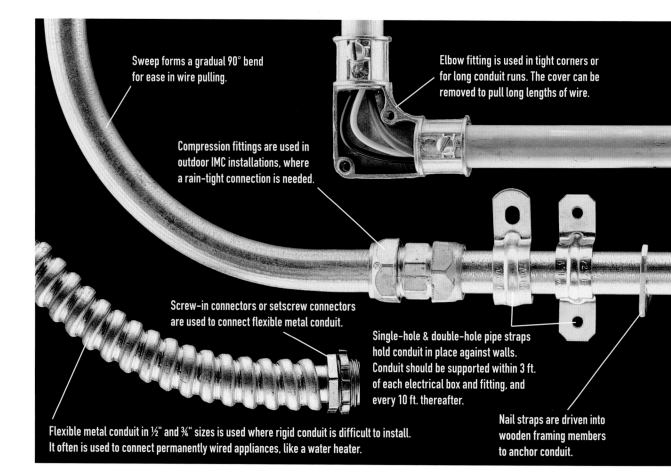

Sweep forms a gradual 90° bend for ease in wire pulling.

Elbow fitting is used in tight corners or for long conduit runs. The cover can be removed to pull long lengths of wire.

Compression fittings are used in outdoor IMC installations, where a rain-tight connection is needed.

Screw-in connectors or setscrew connectors are used to connect flexible metal conduit.

Single-hole & double-hole pipe straps hold conduit in place against walls. Conduit should be supported within 3 ft. of each electrical box and fitting, and every 10 ft. thereafter.

Nail straps are driven into wooden framing members to anchor conduit.

Flexible metal conduit in ½" and ¾" sizes is used where rigid conduit is difficult to install. It often is used to connect permanently wired appliances, like a water heater.

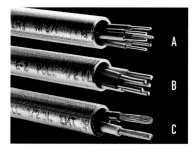

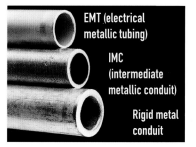

Fill Capacity: Conduit ½" in diameter can hold up to six 14-gauge or 12-gauge thhn/thwn wires (A), five 10-gauge wires (B), or two 8-gauge wires (C). Use ¾" conduit for greater capacity. Local codes may vary—check with your electrical inspector.

Metal Conduit: EMT is lightweight and easy to install. IMC has thicker galvanized walls and is a good choice for exposed outdoor use. Rigid metal conduit provides the greatest protection for wires, but it is more expensive and requires threaded fittings. EMT is the preferred metal conduit for home use.

Plastic Conduit: Plastic PVC conduit is allowed by many local codes. It is assembled with solvent glue and PVC fittings that resemble those for metal conduit. When wiring with PVC conduit, always run a green grounding wire.

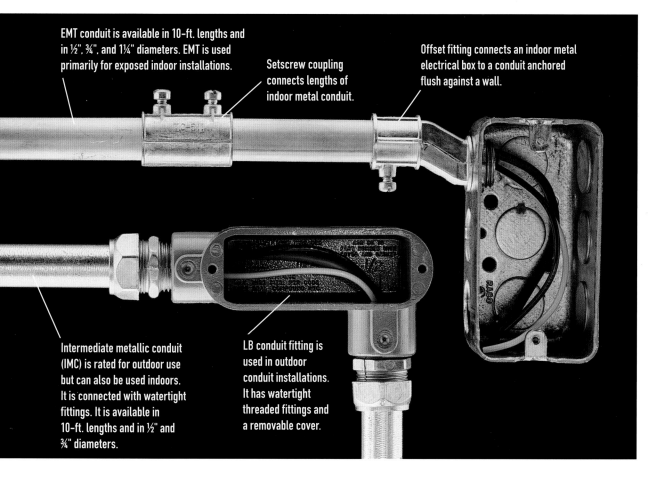

EMT conduit is available in 10-ft. lengths and in ½", ¾", and 1¼" diameters. EMT is used primarily for exposed indoor installations.

Setscrew coupling connects lengths of indoor metal conduit.

Offset fitting connects an indoor metal electrical box to a conduit anchored flush against a wall.

Intermediate metallic conduit (IMC) is rated for outdoor use but can also be used indoors. It is connected with watertight fittings. It is available in 10-ft. lengths and in ½" and ¾" diameters.

LB conduit fitting is used in outdoor conduit installations. It has watertight threaded fittings and a removable cover.

WORK WITH CONDUIT

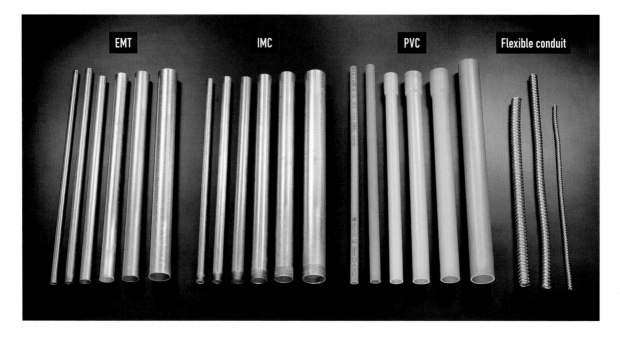

Conduit types used most in homes are EMT (electrical metallic tubing), IMC (intermediate metallic conduit), RNC (rigid nonmetallic conduit), and flexible metal conduit. The most common diameters by far are ½" and ¾", but larger sizes are stocked at most building centers.

Nonmetallic conduit fittings typically are solvent welded to nonmetallic conduit, as opposed to metal conduit, which can be threaded and screwed into threaded fittings or attached with setscrews or compression fittings.

A thin-wall conduit bender is used to bend sweeps into EMT or IMC conduit.

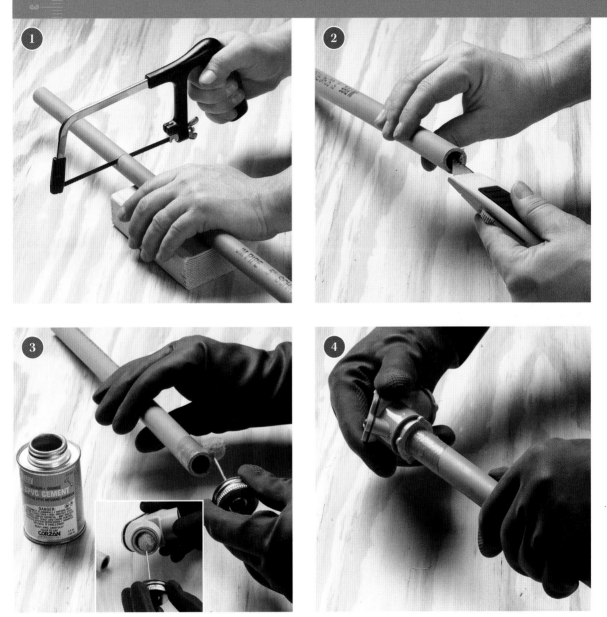

1   Cut the rigid nonmetallic conduit (RNC) to length with a fine-tooth saw, such as a hacksaw. For larger diameter (1½" and above), use a power miter box with a fine-tooth or plastic cutting blade.

2   Deburr the cut edges with a utility knife or fine sandpaper such as emery paper. Wipe the cut ends with a dry rag. Also wipe the coupling or fitting to clean it.

3   Apply a coat of PVC cement to the end of the conduit and to the inside walls of the coupling (inset). Wear latex gloves to protect your hands. The cement should be applied past the point on the conduit where it enters the fitting or coupling.

4   Insert the conduit into the fitting or coupling and spin it a quarter turn to help spread the cement. Allow the joint to set undisturbed for 10 minutes.

ELECTRICAL BOXES

The National Electrical Code requires that wire connections and cable splices be contained inside an approved metal or plastic box. This shields framing members and other flammable materials from electrical sparks.

Electrical boxes come in several shapes. Rectangular and square boxes are used for switches and receptacles. Rectangular (2 × 3") boxes are used for single switches or duplex receptacles. Square (4 × 4") boxes are used any time it is convenient for two switches or receptacles to be wired, or "ganged," in one box, an arrangement common in kitchens or entry hallways. Octagonal electrical boxes contain wire connections for ceiling fixtures.

All electrical boxes are available in different depths. A box must be deep enough so a switch or receptacle can be removed or installed easily without crimping and damaging the circuit wires. Replace an undersized box with a larger box using the Electrical Box Chart (right) as a guide. The NEC also says that all electrical boxes must remain accessible. Never cover an electrical box with drywall, paneling, or wallcoverings.

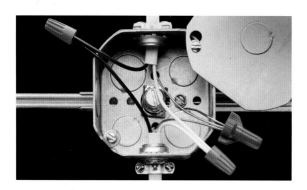

Octagonal boxes usually contain wire connections for ceiling fixtures. Cables are inserted into the box through knockout openings and are held with cable clamps. Because the ceiling fixture attaches directly to the box, the box should be anchored firmly to a framing member. Often, it is nailed directly to a ceiling joist. However, metal braces are available that allow a box to be mounted between joists or studs. A properly installed octagonal box can support a ceiling fixture weighing up to 35 pounds. Any box must be covered with a tightly fitting cover plate, and the box must not have open knockouts.

Electrical Box Fill Chart

BOX SIZE AND SHAPE	MAXIMUM NUMBER OF CONDUCTORS PERMITTED (SEE NOTES BELOW)			
	18 AWG	16 AWG	14 AWG	12 AWG
Junction Boxes				
4 × 1¼" R or O	8	7	6	5
4 × 1½" R or 0	10	8	7	6
4 × 2⅛" R or O	14	12	10	9
4 × 1¼" S	12	10	9	8
4 × 1½" S	14	12	10	9
4 × 2⅛" S	20	17	15	13
4¹¹⁄₁₆ × 1¼" S	17	14	12	11
4¹¹⁄₁₆ × 1½" S	19	16	14	13
4¹¹⁄₁₆ × 2⅛" S	28	24	21	18
Device Boxes				
3 × 2 × 1½"	5	4	3	3
3 × 2 × 2"	6	5	5	4
3 × 2 × 2¼"	7	6	5	4
3 × 2 × 2½"	8	7	6	5
3 × 2 × 2¾"	9	8	7	6
3 × 2 × 3½"	12	10	9	8
4 × 2⅛ × 1½"	6	5	5	4
4 × 2⅛ × 1⅞"	8	7	6	5
4 × 2⅛ × 2⅛"	9	8	7	6

Notes:
- R = Round; O = Octagonal; S = Square or rectangular
- Each hot or neutral wire entering the box is counted as one conductor.
- Grounding wires are counted as one conductor in total—do not count each one individually.
- Raceway fittings and external cable clamps do not count. Internal cable connectors and straps count as either half or one conductor, depending on type.
- Devices (switches and receptacles mainly) each count as two conductors.
- When calculating total conductors, any nonwire components should be assigned the gauge of the largest wire in the box.
- For wire gauges not shown here, contact your local electrical inspections office.

Common Electrical Boxes

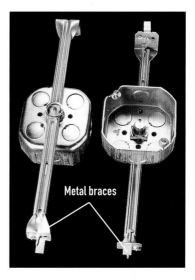

Detachable side

Adapter cover

Metal braces

Rectangular boxes are used with wall switches and duplex receptacles. Single-size rectangular boxes (shown above) may have detachable sides that allow them to be ganged together to form double-size boxes.

Square 4 × 4" boxes are large enough for most wiring applications. They are used for cable splices and ganged receptacles or switches. To install one switch or receptacle in a square box, use an adapter cover.

Braced octagonal boxes fit between ceiling joists. The metal braces extend to fit any joist spacing and are nailed or screwed to framing members.

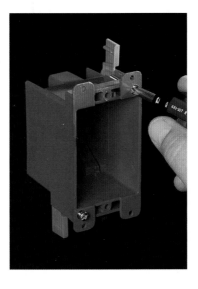

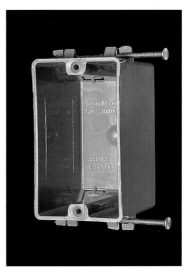

Foam gasket

Outdoor boxes have sealed seams and foam gaskets to guard a switch or receptacle against moisture. Corrosion-resistant coatings protect all metal parts. Code compliant models include a watertight hood.

Retrofit boxes can be installed to upgrade older boxes or to allow you to add new additional receptacles and switches. One type (above) has built-in clamps that tighten against the inside of a wall and hold the box in place.

Plastic boxes are common in new construction. They can be used only with NM (nonmetallic) cable. The box may include preattached nails for anchoring it to framing members. Wall switches must have grounding screws if installed in plastic boxes.

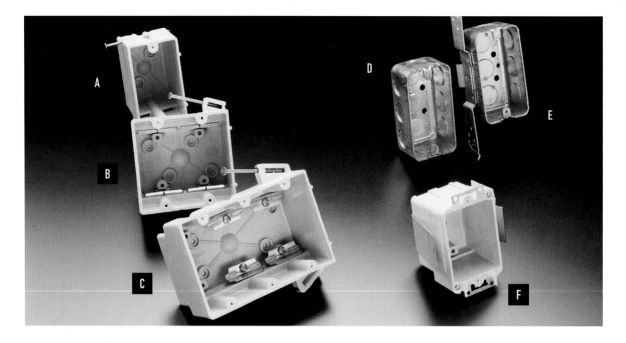

3½"-deep plastic boxes with preattached mounting nails are used for any wiring project protected by finished walls. Common styles include single-gang (A), double-gang (B), and triple-gang (C). Double-gang and triple-gang boxes require internal cable clamps. Metal boxes (D) should be used for exposed indoor wiring, such as conduit installations in an unfinished basement. Metal boxes (E) also can be used for wiring that will be covered by finished walls. Plastic retrofit boxes (F) are used when a new switch or receptacle must fit inside a finished wall. Use internal cable clamps.

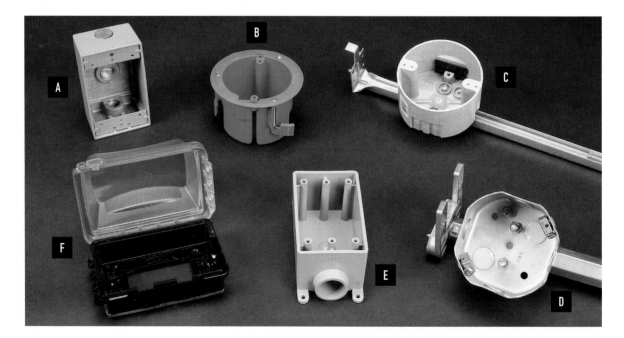

Additional electrical boxes include: Cast aluminum box (A) for use with·outdoor fixtures, including receptacles that are wired through metal conduit. These must have in-use covers if they house receptacles; retrofit ceiling box (B) used for light fixtures; light-duty ceiling fan box (C) with brace that spans ceiling joists; heavy-duty retrofit ceiling fan box (D) designed for retrofit; PVC box (E) for use with PVC conduit in indoor or outdoor setting; wall-mounted in-use cover (F) for exterior receptacle.

Box Specifications

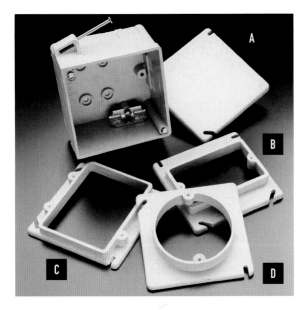

High-quality nonmetallic boxes are rigid and don't contort easily. A variety of adapter plates are available, including junction box cover plate (A), single-gang (B), double-gang (C), and light fixture (D). Adapter plates come in several thicknesses to match different wall constructions.

Boxes larger than 2 × 4" and all retrofit boxes must have internal cable clamps. After installing cables in the box, tighten the cable clamps over the cables so they are gripped firmly, but not so tightly that the cable sheathing is crushed.

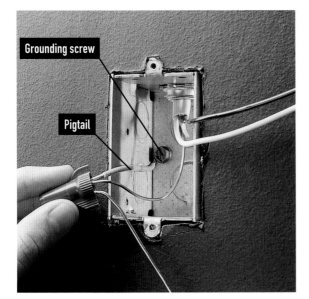

Grounding screw

Pigtail

Metal boxes must be grounded to the circuit grounding system. Connect the circuit grounding wires to the box with a green insulated pigtail wire and wire connector (as shown) or with a grounding clip (page 32).

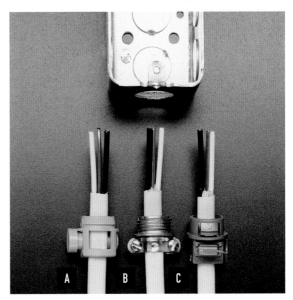

Cables entering a metal box must be clamped. A variety of clamps are available, including plastic clamps (A, C) and threaded metal clamps (B).

Nonmetallic Boxes

Nonmetallic electrical boxes have taken over much of the do-it-yourself market. Most are sold prefitted with installation hardware—from metal wings to 10d common nails attached at the perfect angle for a nail-in box.

In addition to cost and availability, nonmetallic boxes hold a big advantage over metal boxes in that their resistance to conducting electricity will prevent a sparking short circuit if a hot wire contacts the box. Nonmetallic boxes generally are not approved for exposed areas, where they may be susceptible to damage. Their lack of rigidity also allows them to compress or distort, which can reduce the interior capacity beyond code minimums or make outlets difficult to attach.

Low cost is the primary reason that blue PVC nail-in boxes are so popular. Not only are they inexpensive, they also feature built-in cable clamps so you may not need to buy extra hardware to install them. The standard PVC nail-in box is prefitted with a pair of 10d common nails for attaching to exposed wall studs. These boxes, often called handy boxes, are too small to be of much use (see fill chart, page 40).

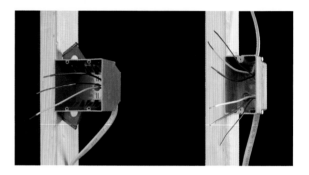

The bulk of the nonmetallic boxes sold today are inexpensive blue PVC. You can also purchase heavier-duty fiberglass or thermoset plastic models that provide a nonmetallic option for installing heavier devices.

Nonmetallic boxes for home use include: Single-gang, double-gang, triple gang, and quad boxes (A); thermoset and fiberglass boxes for heavier duty (B); round fixture boxes (C) for ceiling installation (nail-in and with integral metal bracket).

Tips for Working with Nonmetallic Boxes

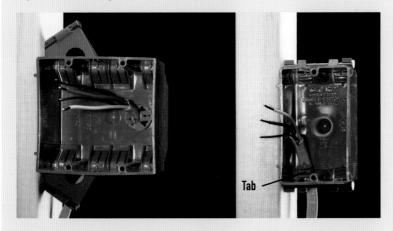

Tab

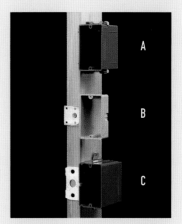

A

B

C

Do not break off the tabs that cover cable entry holes in plastic boxes. These are not knockouts as you would find in metal boxes. In single-gang boxes (right), the pressure from the tab is sufficient to secure the cable as long as it enters with sheathing intact and is stapled no more than 8" from the box. On larger boxes (left), you will find traditional knockouts intended to be used with plastic cable clamps that resemble metal cable clamps. Use these for heavier gauge cable and cable with more than three wires.

Nail-in boxes (A) are prefitted with 10d nails that are attached perpendicular to the face of single-gang boxes and at an inward angle for better gripping power on larger boxes. Side-mount boxes (B) feature a nailing plate that is attached to the front of the stud to automatically create the correct setback; adjustable side-mount boxes (C) are installed the same way but can be moved on the bracket.

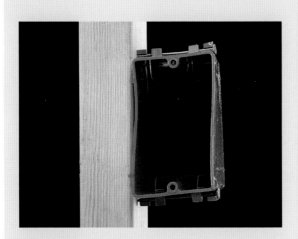

Ribs

Distortion can occur in nonmetallic boxes when nails or other fasteners are overdriven or installed at improper angles, or when the semiflexible boxes are compressed into improperly sized or shaped openings. This can reduce the box capacity and prevent devices and faceplates from fitting.

Integral ribs cast into many nonmetallic boxes are used to register the box against the wall studs so the front edges of the box will be flush with the wall surface after drywall is installed. Most are set for ½" drywall, but if your wall will be a different thickness you may be able to find a box with corresponding ribs. Otherwise, use a piece of the wallcovering material as a reference.

INSTALL BOXES

Install electrical boxes for receptacles, switches, and fixtures only after your wiring project plan has been approved by your inspector. Use your wiring plan as a guide, and follow electrical code height and spacing guidelines when laying out box positions.

Always use the deepest electrical boxes that are practical for your installation. Using deep boxes ensures that you will meet code regulations regarding box volume and makes it easier to make the wire connections.

Some electrical fixtures, like recessed light fixtures, electric heaters, and exhaust fans, have built-in wire connection boxes. Install the frames for these fixtures at the same time you are installing the other electrical boxes.

Electrical boxes in adjacent rooms should be positioned close together when they share a common wall and are controlled by the same circuit. This simplifies the cable installations and also reduces the amount of cable needed.

Fixtures That Do Not Need Electrical Boxes

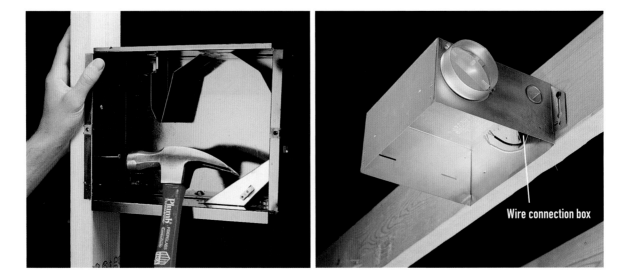

Wire connection box

Recessed fixtures that fit inside wall cavities have built-in wire connection boxes and require no additional electrical boxes. Common recessed fixtures include electric blower-heaters (left), bathroom vent fans (right), and recessed light fixtures. Install the frames for these fixtures at the same time you are installing the other electrical boxes along the circuit. Surface-mounted fixtures like electric baseboard heaters (pages 106 to 109) and under-cabinet fluorescent lights also have built-in wire connection boxes. These fixtures are not installed until it is time to make the final hookups.

INSTALLING ELECTRICAL BOXES FOR RECEPTACLES

Adapter plate

1   Mark the location of each box on studs. Standard receptacle boxes should be centered 12" above floor level. GFCI receptacle boxes in a bathroom should be mounted so they will be about 10" above the finished countertop.

2   Position each box against a stud so the front face will be flush with the finished wall. For example, if you will be installing ½" wallboard, position the box so it extends ½" past the face of the stud. Anchor the box by driving the mounting nails into the stud.

3   If installing square boxes, attach the adapter plates before positioning the boxes. Use adapter plates that match the thickness of the finished wall. Anchor the box by driving the mounting nails into the stud.

4   Open one knockout for each cable that will enter the box, using a hammer and screwdriver. Always introduce the new cable through the knockout that is farthest way from the wall stud.

5   Break off any sharp edges that might damage vinyl cable sheathing by rotating a screwdriver in the knockout.

INSTALLING BOXES FOR LIGHT FIXTURES

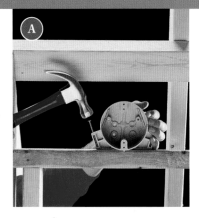
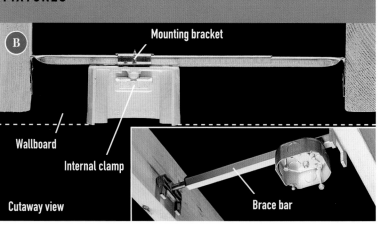

A   Position the light fixture box for a vanity light above the frame opening for a mirror or medicine cabinet. Place the box for a ceiling light fixture in the center of the room. Position each box against a framing member so the front face will be flush with the finished wall or ceiling, then anchor the box by driving the mounting nails into the framing.

B   To position a light fixture between joists, attach an electrical box to an adjustable brace bar. Nail the ends of the brace bar to joists so the face of the box will be flush with the finished ceiling surface. Slide the box along the brace bar to the desired position, then tighten the mounting screws. Use internal cable clamps when using a box with a brace bar. Note: For ceiling fans and heavy fixtures, use a metal box and a heavy-duty brace bar rated for heavy loads (inset photo).

INSTALLING BOXES FOR SWITCHES

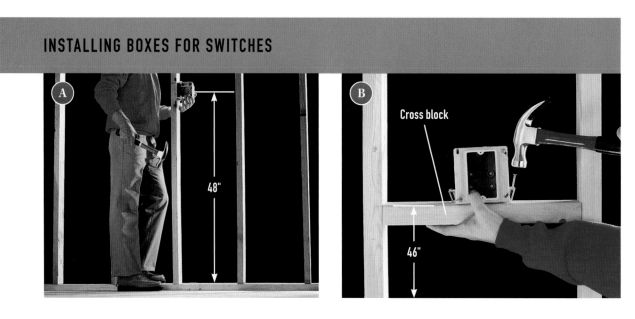

A   Install switch boxes at accessible locations, usually on the latch side of a door, with the center of the box 48" from the floor. The box for a thermostat is mounted at 48" to 60". Position each box against the side of a stud so the front face will be flush with the finished wall, and drive the mounting nails into the stud.

B   To install a switch box between studs, first install a cross block between studs, with the top edge 46" above the floor. Position the box on the cross block so the front face will be flush with the finished wall, and drive the mounting nails into the cross block.

Heights of electrical boxes vary depending on use. In the kitchen shown here, boxes above the countertop are 45" above the floor, in the center of 18" backsplashes that extend from the countertop to the cabinets. All boxes for wall switches also are installed at this height. The center of the box for the microwave receptacle is 72" off the floor. The centers of the boxes for the range and food disposer receptacles are 12" off the floor, but the center of the box for the dishwasher receptacle is 6" off the floor.

Typical Wallcovering Thickness

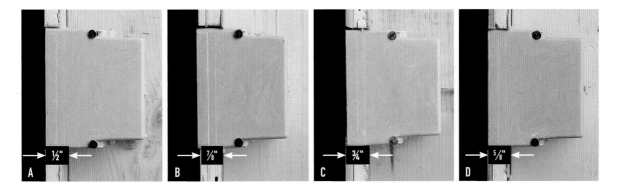

Consider the thickness of finished walls when mounting electrical boxes against framing members. Code requires that the front face of boxes be flush with the finished wall surface, so how you install boxes will vary depending on the type of wall finish that will be used. For example, if the walls will be finished with ½" wallboard (A), attach the boxes so the front faces extend ½" past the front of the framing members. With ceramic tile and wall board (B), extend the boxes ⅞" past the framing members. With ¼" Corian® over wallboard (C), boxes should extend ¾"; and with wallboard and laminate (D), boxes extend ⅝".

Ceiling Boxes

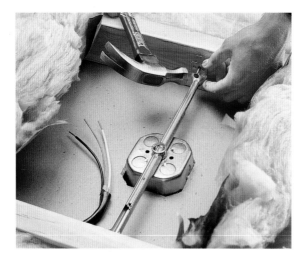

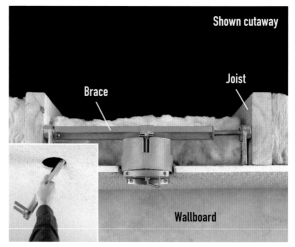

Ceiling boxes for lights are generally round or octagonal in shape to fit typical lamp mounting plates. The easiest way to install one is by nailing the brace to open ceiling joists from above. If the ceiling is insulated, pull the insulation away from the box if the fixture you're installing is not rated IC for insulation contact.

A heavy-duty brace is required for anchoring boxes that will support heavy chandeliers and ceiling fans. A remodeling brace like the one seen here is designed to install through a small cutout in the ceiling (inset photo).

INSTALLING A JUNCTION BOX

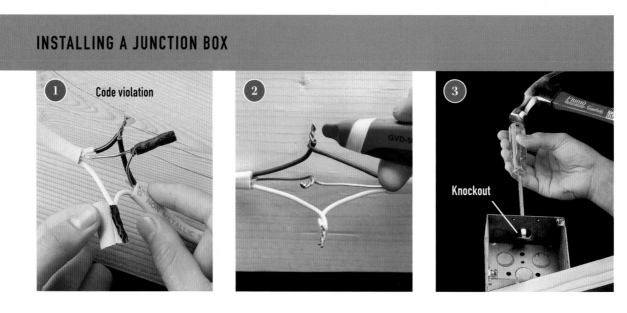

1   Turn off power to circuit wires at the main service panel. Carefully remove any tape or wire connectors from the exposed splice. Avoid contact with the bare wire ends until the wires have been tested for power.

2   Test for power. The tester should not glow. If it does, the wires are still hot. Shut off power to the correct circuit at the main service panel. Disconnect the illegally spliced wires.

3   Open one knockout for each cable that will enter the box, using a hammer and screwdriver.

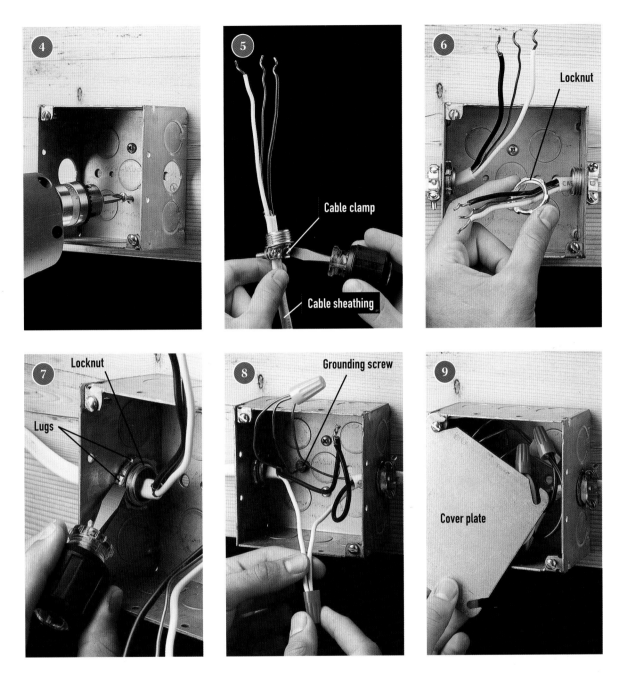

4   Anchor the electrical box to a wooden framing member using screws or nails.

5   Thread each cable end through a cable clamp. Tighten the clamp with a screwdriver. See if there is any slack in the cables so you can gain a little extra cable to work with.

6   Insert the cables into the electrical box, and screw a locknut onto each cable clamp.

7   Tighten the locknuts by pushing against the lugs with the blade of a screwdriver.

8   Use wire connectors to reconnect the wires. Pigtail the copper grounding wires to the green grounding screw in the back of the box.

9   Carefully tuck the wires into the box, and attach the cover plate. Turn on the power to the circuit at the main service panel. Make sure the box remains accessible and is not concealed by finished walls or ceilings.

Install Pop-in Retrofit Boxes

Attaching an electrical box to a wall stud during new construction is relatively easy. The task becomes complicated, however, when you're working in finished walls during remodeling or repair. In most cases, it's best to use an electronic stud finder, make a large cutout in the wall, and attach a new box directly to a framing member or bracing (and then replace and refinish the wall materials). But there are occasions when this isn't possible or practical and you just need to retrofit an electrical box without making a large hole in the wall. You also may find that an older switch or receptacle box is too shallow to accommodate a new dimmer or GFCI safely. These situations call for a pop-in retrofit box (sometimes called an "old work" box).

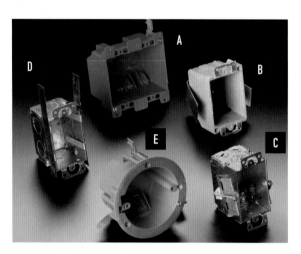

Tools & Materials	
Screwdriver	Template (if provided)
Pencil	Plastic or metal
String	pop-in box
Electrical tape	Eye protection
Wallboard saw	

Pop-in boxes for remodeling come in variety of styles. For walls, they include plastic retrofit boxes with flip-out wings (A), metal or plastic boxes with compression tabs or brackets (B), metal retrofit boxes with flip-out wings (C), and metal boxes with bendable brackets, also known as F-straps, (D). For ceilings, plastic fixture boxes with flip-out wings (E) are available.

REMOVING AN ELECTRICAL BOX

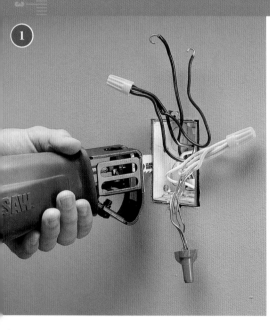

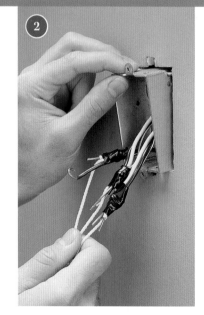

1   To install a dimmer switch or GFCI receptacle, you may have to replace an old, overcrowded box. Shut off power and remove the old switch or receptacle. Identify the location of nails holding the box to the framing member and cut the nails with a hacksaw or reciprocating saw with a metal blade inserted between the box and the stud.

2   Bind the cable ends together and attach string in case they fall into the wall cavity when the old box is removed. Disconnect the cable clamps and slide the old box out. Install a new pop-in box (see next page).

INSTALLING A POP-IN BOX

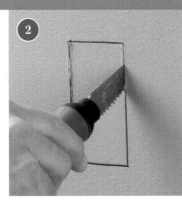

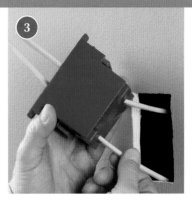

Flip-out wings

Back of wall

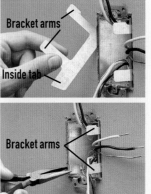

Bracket arms

Inside tab

Bracket arms

Variation: Feed cable into the new box and secure it in the opening after clamping the cables. With this pop-in box, bracket arms are inserted at the sides of the box (top) and then bent around the front edges to secure the box in the opening (bottom).

1   Use a template to trace a cutout for the box at the intended location. If no template is provided, press the pop-in box against the wall surface and trace its front edges (but not the tabs on the top and bottom).

2   Puncture the wallboard with the tip of a wallboard saw or by drilling a small hole inside the lines, and make the cutout for the box.

3   Pull NM cable through a knockout in the box (no cable clamp is required with a plastic box; just be sure not to break the pressure tab that holds the cable in place).

4   Insert the box into the cutout so the tabs are flush against the wall surface. Tighten the screws that cause the flip-out wings to pivot (right) until the box is held firmly in place. Connect the switch or receptacle that the box will house.

ELECTRICAL PANELS

Every home has a main service panel that distributes electrical current to the individual circuits. The main service panel usually is found in the basement, garage, or utility area, and can be identified by its metal casing. Before making any repair to your electrical system, you must shut off power to the correct circuit at the main service panel. The service panel should be indexed (page 7) so circuits can be identified easily.

Service panels vary in appearance, depending on the age of the system. Very old wiring may operate on 30-amp service that has only two circuits. New homes can have 200-amp service with 30 or more circuits. Find the size of the service by reading the amperage rating printed on the main fuse block or main circuit breaker.

Regardless of age, all service panels have fuses or circuit breakers that control each circuit and protect them from overloads. In general, older service panels use fuses, while newer service panels use circuit breakers.

In addition to the main service panel, your electrical system may have a subpanel that controls some of the circuits in the home. A subpanel has its own circuit breakers or fuses and is installed to control circuits that have been added to an existing wiring system.

The subpanel resembles the main service panel but is usually smaller. It may be located near the main panel, or it may be found near the areas served by the new circuits. Garages and basements that have been updated often have their own subpanels. If your home has a subpanel, make sure that its circuits are indexed correctly.

When handling fuses or circuit breakers, make sure the area around the service panel is dry. Never remove the protective cover on the service panel. After turning off a circuit to make electrical repairs, remember to always test the circuit for power before touching any wires.

The main service panel is the heart of your wiring system. As our demand for household energy has increased, the panels have also grown in capacity. Today, a 200-amp panel is considered the minimum for new construction.

Tip

Every house should have a properly labeled service panel. This makes it much easier to find a circuit that has been tripped. If the same circuit is regularly tripped, you are either overloading the circuit, or there is a problem with the wiring or the circuit breaker.

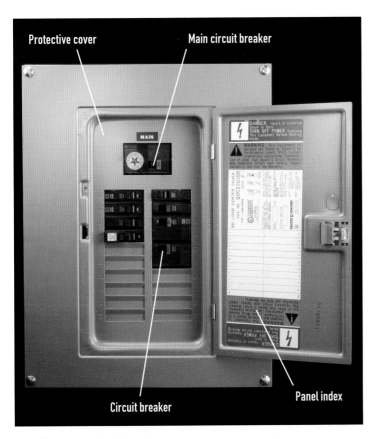

Protective cover

Main circuit breaker

Circuit breaker

Panel index

A circuit breaker panel providing 100 amps or more of power is common in wiring systems installed during the 1960s and later. A circuit breaker panel is housed in a gray metal cabinet that contains two rows of individual circuit breakers. The size of the service can be identified by reading the amperage rating of the main circuit breaker, which is located at the top or bottom of the main service panel.

A 200-amp service panel is now the minimum standard for all new housing. It is considered adequate for a medium-sized house with no more than three major electric appliances. However, larger houses with more electrical appliances often are equipped with a 400-amp service panel.

To shut off power to individual circuits in a circuit breaker panel, flip the lever on the appropriate circuit breaker to the OFF position. To shut off the power to the entire house, turn the main circuit breaker to the OFF position.

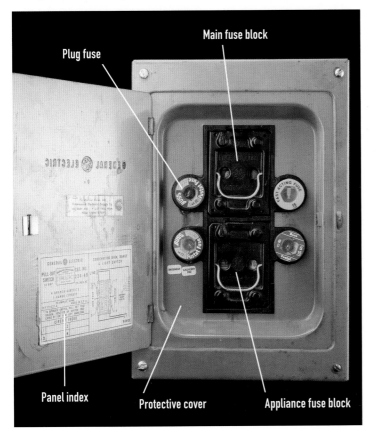

Plug fuse

Main fuse block

Panel index

Protective cover

Appliance fuse block

A 60-amp fuse panel often is found in wiring systems installed between 1950 and 1965. It usually is housed in a gray metal cabinet that contains four individual plug fuses, plus one or two pull-out fuse blocks that hold cartridge fuses. This type of panel is regarded as adequate for a small, 1,100-sq. ft. house that has no more than one 240-volt appliance. Many homeowners update 60-amp service to 100 amps or more so that additional lighting and appliance circuits can be added to the system. Home loan programs also may require that 60-amp service be updated before a home can qualify for financing.

To shut off power to a circuit, carefully unscrew the plug fuse, touching only its insulated rim. To shut off power to the entire house, hold the handle of the main fuse block and pull sharply to remove it. Major appliance circuits are controlled with another cartridge fuse block. Shut off the appliance circuit by pulling out this fuse block.

Circuit Breaker Panels

The circuit breaker panel is the electrical distribution center for your home. It divides the current into branch circuits that are carried throughout the house. Each branch circuit is controlled by a circuit breaker that protects the wires from dangerous current overloads. When installing new circuits, the last step is to connect the wires to new circuit breakers at the panel. Working inside a circuit breaker panel is not dangerous if you follow basic safety procedures. Always shut off the main circuit breaker and test for power before touching any parts inside the panel, and never touch the service wire lugs. If unsure of your own skills, hire an electrician to make the final circuit connections. (If you have an older electrical service with fuses instead of circuit breakers, always have an electrician make these final hookups.)

Main circuit breaker panel distributes the power entering the home into branch circuits.

Neutral service wire carries current back to the power source after it has passed through the home.

Two hot service wires provide 120/240 volts of power to the main circuit breaker. These wires are always HOT.

Main circuit breaker protects the hot service wires from overloads and transfers power to two hot bus bars.

Double-pole breaker wired for a 120/240 circuit transfers power from the two hot bus bars to red and black hot wires in a three-wire cable.

Neutral bus bar has setscrew terminals for linking all neutral circuit wires to the neutral service wire.

Slimline circuit breakers require half as much space as standard single-pole breakers. Slimlines can be used to make room for added circuits.

Service wire lugs: DO NOT TOUCH

Grounding bus bar has terminals for linking grounding wires to the main grounding conductor. It is bonded to the neutral bus bar.

120-volt branch circuits

Subpanel feeder breaker is a double-pole breaker, usually 30 to 50 amps. It is wired in the same way as a 120/240-volt circuit.

Two hot bus bars run through the center of the panel, supplying power to the circuit breakers. Each carries 120 volts.

Grounding conductor leads to metal grounding rods driven into the earth.

120/240-volt branch circuit

If the main circuit breaker panel does not have enough open slots to hold new circuit breakers, install a subpanel. This job is well within the skill level of an experienced do-it-yourselfer, although you can also hire an electrician to install the subpanel.

Before installing any new wiring, evaluate your electrical service to make sure it provides enough current to support both the existing wiring and any new circuits. If your service does not provide enough power, have an electrician upgrade it to a higher amp rating. During the upgrade, the electrician will install a new circuit breaker panel with enough extra breaker slots for the new circuits you want to install.

Safety Warning

Never touch any parts inside a circuit breaker panel until you have checked for power. Circuit breaker panels differ in appearance, depending on the manufacturer. Never begin work in a circuit breaker panel until you understand its layout and can identify the parts.

Circuit breaker subpanel can be installed when the main circuit breaker panel does not have enough space to hold circuit breakers for new circuits you want to install. Two hot feeder wires supply 120 volts of power to the two hot bus bars.

Neutral feeder wire connects the neutral bus bar in the subpanel to the neutral bus bar in the main service panel.

Neutral bus bar has setscrew terminals for linking neutral circuit wires to the neutral feed wire.

Single-pole circuit breaker transfers 120 volts of power from one hot bus bar to the black hot wire in a two-wire cable.

Grounding bus bar has setscrew terminals for connecting circuit grounding wires. In a circuit breaker subpanel, the grounding bus bar is not bonded to the neutral bus bar.

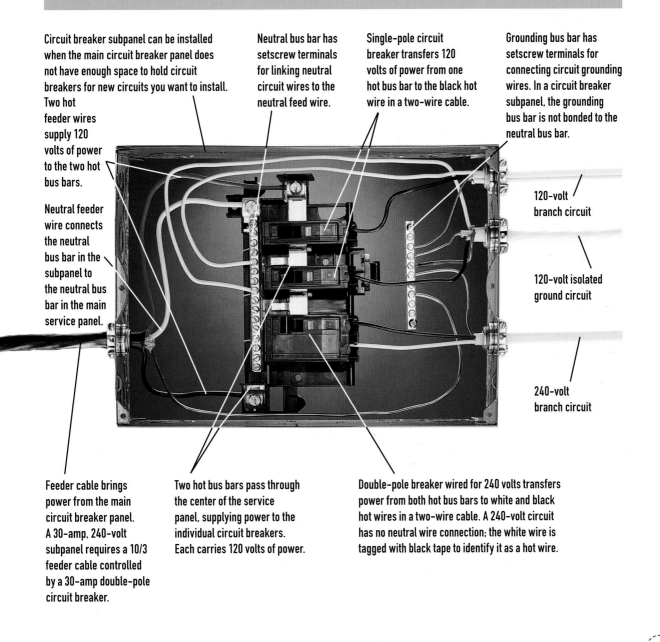

120-volt branch circuit

120-volt isolated ground circuit

240-volt branch circuit

Feeder cable brings power from the main circuit breaker panel. A 30-amp, 240-volt subpanel requires a 10/3 feeder cable controlled by a 30-amp double-pole circuit breaker.

Two hot bus bars pass through the center of the service panel, supplying power to the individual circuit breakers. Each carries 120 volts of power.

Double-pole breaker wired for 240 volts transfers power from both hot bus bars to white and black hot wires in a two-wire cable. A 240-volt circuit has no neutral wire connection; the white wire is tagged with black tape to identify it as a hot wire.

Fuses & Circuit Breakers

Fuses and circuit breakers are safety devices designed to protect the electrical system from short circuits and overloads. Fuses and circuit breakers are located in the main service panel.

Most service panels installed before 1965 rely on fuses to control and protect individual circuits. Screw-in plug fuses protect 120-volt circuits that power lights and receptacles. Cartridge fuses protect 240-volt appliance circuits and the main shutoff of the service panel.

Inside each fuse is a current-carrying metal alloy ribbon. If a circuit is overloaded, the metal ribbon melts and stops the flow of power. A fuse must match the amperage rating of the circuit. Never replace a fuse with one that has a larger amperage rating.

In most service panels installed after 1965, circuit breakers protect and control individual circuits. Single-pole circuit breakers protect 120-volt circuits, and double-pole circuit breakers protect 240-volt circuits. Amperage ratings for circuit breakers range from 15 to 100 amps.

Each circuit breaker has a permanent metal strip that heats up and bends when voltage passes through it. If a circuit is overloaded, the metal strip inside the breaker bends enough to "trip" the switch and stop the flow of power. Circuit breakers are listed to trip twice. After the second trip they weaken and tend to nuisance trip at lower currents. Replace breakers that have tripped more than twice—they may fail. Worn circuit breakers should be replaced by an electrician.

When a fuse blows or a circuit breaker trips, it is usually because there are too many light fixtures and plug-in appliances drawing power through the circuit. Move some of the plug-in appliances to another circuit, then replace the fuse or reset the breaker. If the fuse blows or the breaker trips again immediately, there may be a short circuit in the system. Call a licensed electrician if you suspect a short circuit.

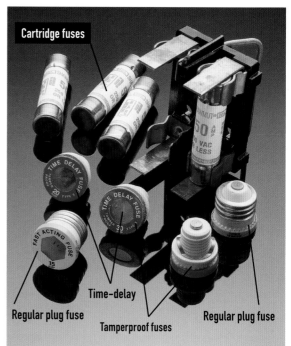

Cartridge fuses

Time-delay

Regular plug fuse

Tamperproof fuses

Regular plug fuse

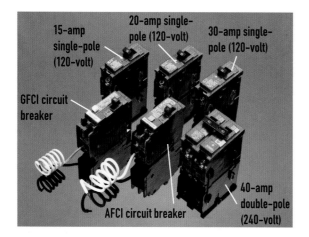

15-amp single-pole (120-volt)

20-amp single-pole (120-volt)

30-amp single-pole (120-volt)

GFCI circuit breaker

AFCI circuit breaker

40-amp double-pole (240-volt)

Circuit breakers are found in the majority of panels installed since the 1940s. Single-pole breakers control 120-volt circuits. Double-pole breakers rated for 20 to 60 amps control 240-volt circuits. Ground-fault circuit interrupter (GFCI) and arc-fault circuit interrupter (AFCI) breakers provide protection from shocks and fire-causing arcs for the entire circuit.

Fuses are used in older service panels. Plug fuses usually control 120-volt circuits rated for 15, 20, or 30 amps. Tamper-proof plug fuses have threads that fit only matching sockets, making it impossible to install a wrong-sized fuse. Time-delay fuses absorb temporary heavy power loads without blowing. Cartridge fuses control 240-volt circuits and range from 30 to 100 amps.

IDENTIFYING & REPLACING A BLOWN PLUG FUSE

1   Locate the blown fuse at the main service panel. If the metal ribbon inside is cleanly melted (right), the circuit was overloaded. If window is discolored (left), there was a short circuit.

2   Unscrew the fuse, being careful to touch only the insulated rim of the fuse. Replace it with a fuse that has the same amperage rating.

REMOVING, TESTING & REPLACING A CARTRIDGE FUSE

1   Remove cartridge fuses by gripping the handle of the fuse block and pulling sharply.

2   Remove the individual cartridge fuses from the block using a fuse puller.

3   Test each fuse using a continuity tester. If the tester glows, the fuse is good. If not, install a new fuse with the same amperage rating.

RESETTING A CIRCUIT BREAKER

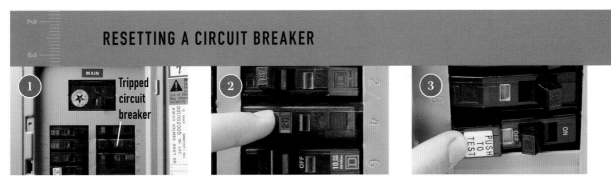

1   Open the service panel and locate the tripped breaker. The lever on the tripped breaker will be either in the OFF position, or in a position between ON and OFF.

2   Reset the tripped circuit breaker by pressing the circuit breaker lever all the way to the OFF position, then pressing it to the ON position.

3   Test AFCI and GFCI circuit breakers by pushing the TEST button. The breaker should trip to the OFF position. If not, the breaker is faulty and must be replaced by an electrician.

Connecting Circuit Breakers

The last step in a wiring project is connecting circuits at the breaker panel. After this is done, the work is ready for the final inspection.

Circuits are connected at the main breaker panel, if it has enough open slots, or at a circuit breaker subpanel. When working at a subpanel, make sure the feeder breaker at the main panel has been turned off, and test for power (photo, right) before touching any parts in the subpanel.

Make sure the circuit breaker amperage does not exceed the ampacity of the circuit wires you are connecting to it. Also be aware that circuit breaker styles and installation techniques vary according to manufacturer. Use breakers designed for your type of panel. For most rooms in a home, in addition to the kitchen, basement, and bathroom, an AFCI breaker needs to be installed.

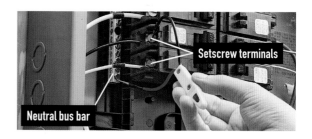

Test for current before touching any parts inside a circuit breaker panel. With main breaker turned off but all other breakers turned on, touch one probe of a neon tester to the neutral bus bar, and touch the other probe to each setscrew on one of the double-pole breakers (not the main breaker). If tester does not light for either setscrew, it is safe to work in the panel. Note: Touchless circuit testers are preferred in most situations where you are testing for current because they're safer. But in some instances you'll need a tester with individual probes to properly check for current.

Tools & Materials

Screwdriver	Pencil	Cable ripper	Pliers	Single- and double-pole
Hammer	Combination tool	Circuit tester	Cable clamps	circuit breakers

CONNECTING CIRCUIT BREAKERS

1   Shut off the main circuit breaker in the main circuit breaker panel (if you are working in a subpanel, shut off the feeder breaker in the main panel). Remove the panel cover plate, taking care not to touch the parts inside the panel. Test for power (photo, top).

2   Open a knockout in the side of the circuit breaker panel using a screwdriver and hammer. Attach a cable clamp to the knockout.

3   Hold cable across the front of the panel near the knockout, and mark sheathing about ½" inside the edge of the panel. Strip the cable from the marked line to the end using a cable ripper. (There should be 18 to 24" of excess cable.) Insert the cable through the clamp and into the service panel, then tighten the clamp.

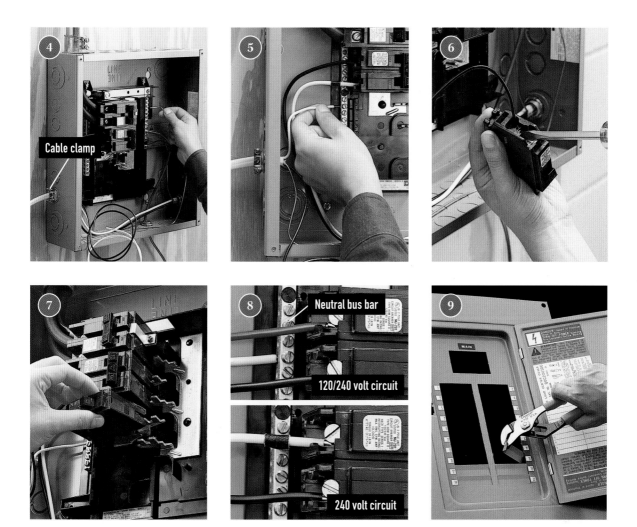

4   Bend the bare copper grounding wire around the inside edge of the panel to an open setscrew terminal on the grounding bus bar. Insert the wire into the opening on the bus bar, and tighten the setscrew. Fold excess wire around the inside edge of the panel.

5   For 120-volt circuits, bend the white circuit wire around the outside of the panel to an open setscrew terminal on the neutral bus bar. Clip away excess wire, then strip ½" of insulation from the wire using a combination tool. Insert the wire into the terminal opening, and tighten the setscrew.

6   Strip ½" of insulation from the end of the black circuit wire. Insert the wire into the setscrew terminal on a new single-pole circuit breaker, and tighten the setscrew.

7   Slide one end of the circuit breaker onto the guide hook, then press it firmly against the bus bar until it snaps into place. (Breaker installation may vary, depending on the manufacturer.) Fold excess black wire around the inside edge of the panel.

8   120/240-volt circuits (top): Connect red and black wires to the double-pole breaker. Connect white wire to the neutral bus bar, and grounding wire to the grounding bus bar. For 240-volt circuits (bottom), attach white and black wires to the double-pole breaker, tagging white wire with black tape. There is no neutral bus bar connection on this circuit.

9   Remove the appropriate breaker knockout on the panel cover plate to make room for the new circuit breaker. A single-pole breaker requires one knockout, while a double-pole breaker requires two knockouts. Reattach the cover plate, and label the new circuit on the panel index.

WALL SWITCHES

An average wall switch is turned on and off more than 1,000 times each year. Because switches receive constant use, wire connections can loosen and switch parts gradually wear out. If a switch no longer operates smoothly, it must be repaired or replaced.

The methods for repairing or replacing a switch vary slightly, depending on the switch type and its location along an electrical circuit. When working on a switch, use the photographs on pages 64 to 67 to identify your switch type and its wiring configuration. Individual switch styles may vary from manufacturer to manufacturer, but the basic switch types are universal.

It is possible to replace most ordinary wall switches with a specialty switch, like a timer switch or an electronic switch. When installing a specialty switch, make sure it is compatible with the wiring configuration of the switch box.

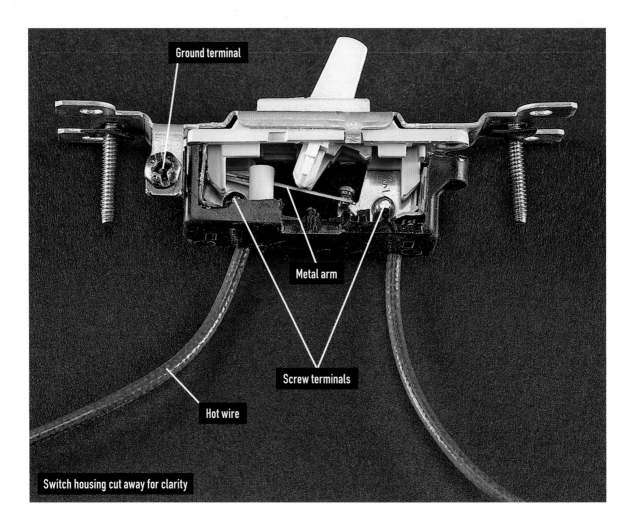

Ground terminal

Metal arm

Screw terminals

Hot wire

Switch housing cut away for clarity

A typical wall switch has a movable metal arm that opens and closes the electrical circuit. When the switch is ON, the arm completes the circuit and power flows between the screw terminals and through the black hot wire to the light fixture. When the switch is OFF, the arm lifts away to interrupt the circuit, and no power flows. Switch problems can occur if the screw terminals are not tight or if the metal arm inside the switch wears out. The switch above has had part of its housing removed so the interior workings can be seen. Switches or fixtures that are not in original condition should never be installed.

Rotary snap switches are found in many installations completed between 1900 and 1920. The handle is twisted clockwise to turn light on and off. The switch is enclosed in a ceramic housing.

Push-button switches were widely used from 1920 until about 1940. Many switches of this type are still in operation. Reproductions of this switch type are available for restoration projects.

Toggle switches were introduced in the 1930s. This early design has a switch mechanism that is mounted in a ceramic housing sealed with a layer of insulating paper.

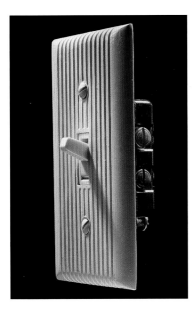

Toggle switches were improved during the 1950s and are now the most commonly used type. This switch type was the first to use a sealed plastic housing that protects the inner switch mechanism from dust and moisture.

Mercury switches became common in the early 1960s. They conduct electrical current by means of a sealed vial of mercury. No longer manufactured for home use, old mercury switches are considered a hazardous waste.

Electronic motion-sensor switches have an infrared eye that senses movement and automatically turns on lights when a person enters a room. Motion-sensor switches can provide added security against intruders.

TYPES OF WALL SWITCHES

Wall switches are available in three general types. To repair or replace a switch, it is important to identify its type.

Single-pole switches are used to control a set of lights from one location. Three-way switches are used to control a set of lights from two different locations and are always installed in pairs. Four-way switches are used in combination with a pair of three-way switches to control a set of lights from three or more locations.

Identify switch types by counting the screw terminals. Single-pole switches have two screw terminals, three-way switches have three screw terminals, and four-way switches have four. Most switches include a grounding screw terminal, which is identified by its green color.

When replacing a switch, choose a new switch that has the same number of screw terminals as the old one. The location of the screws on the switch body varies depending on the manufacturer, but these differences will not affect the switch operation.

Whenever possible, connect switches using the screw terminals rather than push-in fittings. Some specialty switches have wire leads instead of screw terminals. They are connected to circuit wires with wire connectors.

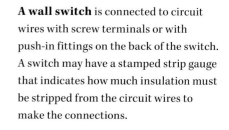

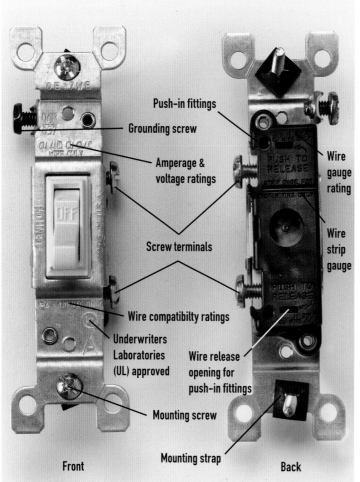

Push-in fittings
Grounding screw
Amperage & voltage ratings
Screw terminals
Wire compatibilty ratings
Underwriters Laboratories (UL) approved
Wire release opening for push-in fittings
Mounting screw
Mounting strap

Wire gauge rating
Wire strip gauge

Front

Back

A wall switch is connected to circuit wires with screw terminals or with push-in fittings on the back of the switch. A switch may have a stamped strip gauge that indicates how much insulation must be stripped from the circuit wires to make the connections.

The switch body is attached to a metal mounting strap that allows it to be mounted in an electrical box. Several rating stamps are found on the strap and on the back of the switch. The abbreviation UL or UND LAB INC LIST means that the switch meets the safety standards of the Underwriters Laboratories. Switches also are stamped with maximum voltage and amperage ratings. Standard wall switches are rated 15A or 125V. Voltage ratings of 110, 120, and 125 are considered to be identical for purposes of identification.

For standard wall switch installations, choose a switch that has a wire gauge rating of #12 or #14. For wire systems with solid-core copper wiring, use only switches marked COPPER or CU. For aluminum wiring, use only switches marked CO/ALR. Switches marked AL/CU can no longer be used with aluminum wiring, according to the National Electrical Code.

Single-Pole Wall Switches

A single-pole switch is the most common type of wall switch. It has ON-OFF markings on the switch lever and is used to control a set of lights, an appliance, or a receptacle from a single location. A single-pole switch has two screw terminals and a grounding screw. When installing a single-pole switch, check to make sure the ON marking shows when the switch lever is in the up position.

In a correctly wired single-pole switch, a hot circuit wire is attached to each screw terminal. However, the color and number of wires inside the switch box will vary, depending on the location of the switch along the electrical circuit.

If two cables enter the box, then the switch lies in the middle of the circuit. In this installation, both of the hot wires attached to the switch are black.

If only one cable enters the box, then the switch lies at the end of the circuit. In this installation (sometimes called a switch loop), one of the hot wires is black, but the other hot wire usually is white. A white hot wire should be coded with black tape or paint.

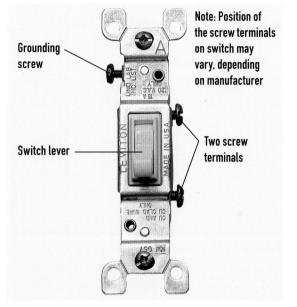

Grounding screw

Switch lever

Note: Position of the screw terminals on switch may vary, depending on manufacturer

Two screw terminals

A single-pole switch is essentially an interruption in the black power supply wire that is opened or closed with the toggle. Single-pole switches are the simplest of all home wiring switches.

Typical Single-Pole Switch Installations

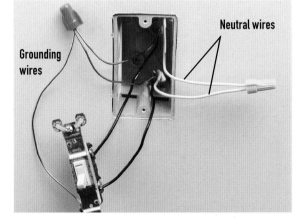

Grounding wires

Neutral wires

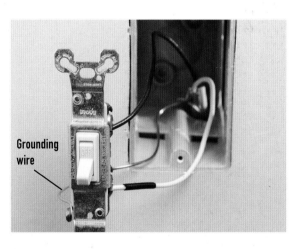

Grounding wire

Two cables enter the box when a switch is located in the middle of a circuit. Each cable has a white and a black insulated wire, plus a bare copper grounding wire. The black wires are hot and are connected to the screw terminals on the switch. The white wires are neutral and are joined together with a wire connector. Grounding wires are pigtailed to the switch.

One cable enters the box when a switch is located at the end of a circuit. The cable has a white and a black insulated wire, plus a bare copper grounding wire. In this installation, both of the insulated wires are hot. The white wire may be labeled with black tape or paint to identify it as a hot wire. The grounding wire is connected to the switch grounding screw.

Three-way Wall Switches

Three-way switches have three screw terminals and do not have ON-OFF markings. Three-way switches are always installed in pairs and are used to control a set of lights from two locations.

One of the screw terminals on a three-way switch is darker than the others. This screw is the common screw terminal. The position of the common screw terminal on the switch body may vary, depending on the manufacturer. Before disconnecting a three-way switch, always label the wire that is connected to the common screw terminal. It must be reconnected to the common screw terminal on the new switch.

The two, lighter-colored screw terminals on a three-way switch are called the traveler screw terminals. The traveler terminals are interchangeable, so there is no need to label the wires attached to them.

Because three-way switches are installed in pairs, it is sometimes difficult to determine which of the switches is causing a problem. The switch that receives greater use is more likely to fail, but you may need to inspect both switches to find the source of the problem.

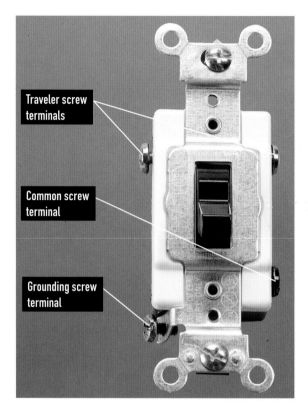

Typical Three-way Switch Installations

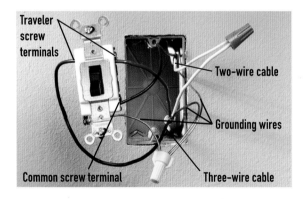

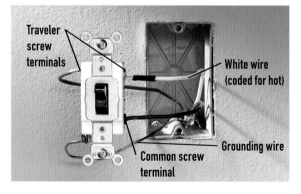

Two cables enter the box if the switch lies in the middle of a circuit. One cable has two wires, plus a bare copper grounding wire; the other cable has three wires, plus a ground. The black wire from the two-wire cable is connected to the dark common screw terminal. The red and black wires from the three-wire cable are connected to the traveler screw terminals. The white neutral wires are joined together with a wire connector, and the grounding wires are pigtailed to the grounded metal box.

One cable enters the box if the switch lies at the end of the circuit. The cable has a black wire, red wire, and white wire, plus a bare copper grounding wire. The black wire must be connected to the common screw terminal, which is darker than the other two screw terminals. The white and red wires are connected to the two traveler screw terminals. The white wire is taped to indicate that it is hot. The bare copper grounding wire is connected to the grounded metal box.

FIXING OR REPLACING A THREE-WAY WALL SWITCH

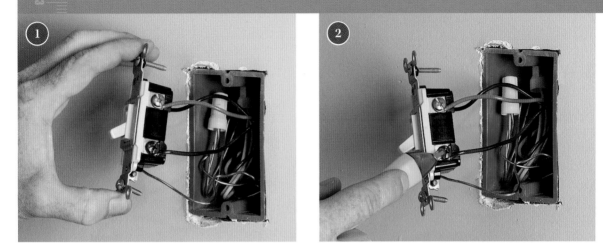

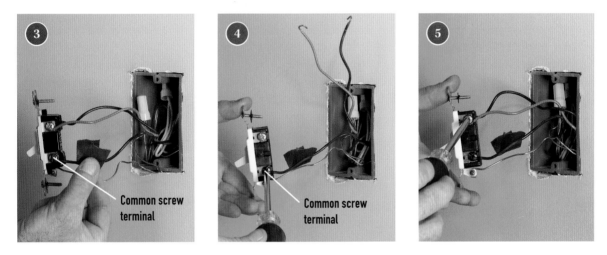

1   Turn off the power to the switch at the main service panel, then remove the switch cover plate and mounting screws. Holding the mounting strap carefully, pull the switch from the box. Be careful not to touch the bare wires or screw terminals until they have been tested for power.

2   Test for power by touching one probe of the circuit tester to the grounded metal box or to the bare copper grounding wire, and touching the other probe to each screw terminal. Tester should not glow. If it does, there is still power entering the box. Return to the service panel, and turn off the correct circuit.

3   Locate the dark common screw terminal, and use masking tape to label the "common" wire attached to it. Disconnect wires and remove the switch. Test the switch for continuity. If it tests faulty, buy a replacement. Inspect wires for nicks and scratches. If necessary, clip damaged wires and strip them.

4   Connect the common wire to the dark common screw terminal on the switch. On most three-way switches, the common screw terminal is black. Or it may be labeled with the word COMMON stamped on the back of the switch. Reconnect the grounding screw; connect it to the circuit grounding wires with a pigtail.

5   Connect the remaining two circuit wires to the screw terminals. These wires are interchangeable and can be connected to either screw terminal. Carefully tuck the wires into the box. Remount the switch, and attach the cover plate. Turn on the power at the main service panel.

Dimmer Switches

A dimmer switch makes it possible to vary the brightness of a light fixture. Dimmers are often installed in dining rooms, recreation areas, or bedrooms.

Any standard single-pole switch can be replaced with a dimmer, as long as the switch box is of adequate size. Dimmer switches have larger bodies than standard switches. They also generate a small amount of heat that must dissipate. For these reasons, dimmers should not be installed in undersized electrical boxes or in boxes that are crowded with circuit wires. Always follow the manufacturer's specifications for installation.

In lighting configurations that use three-way switches (pages 66 to 67), replace the standard switches with special three-way dimmers. If replacing both the switches with dimmers, buy a packaged pair of three-way dimmers designed to work together.

Dimmer switches are available in several styles (photo, right). All types have wire leads instead of screw terminals, and they are connected to circuit wires using wire connectors. Some types have a green grounding lead that should be connected to the grounded metal box or to the bare copper grounding wires.

Tools & Materials
Screwdriver
Circuit tester
Needlenose pliers
Wire connectors
Masking tape

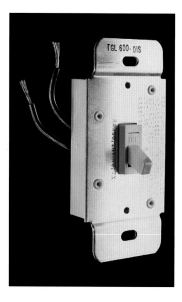

Toggle-type dimmer resembles standard switches. Toggle dimmers are available in both single-pole and three-way designs.

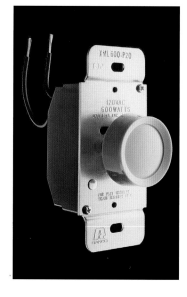

Dial-type dimmer is the most common style. Rotating the dial changes the light intensity.

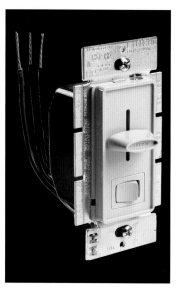

Slide-action dimmer has an illuminated face that makes the switch easy to locate in the dark.

Automatic dimmer has an electronic sensor that adjusts the light fixture to compensate for the changing levels of natural light. An automatic dimmer also can be operated manually.

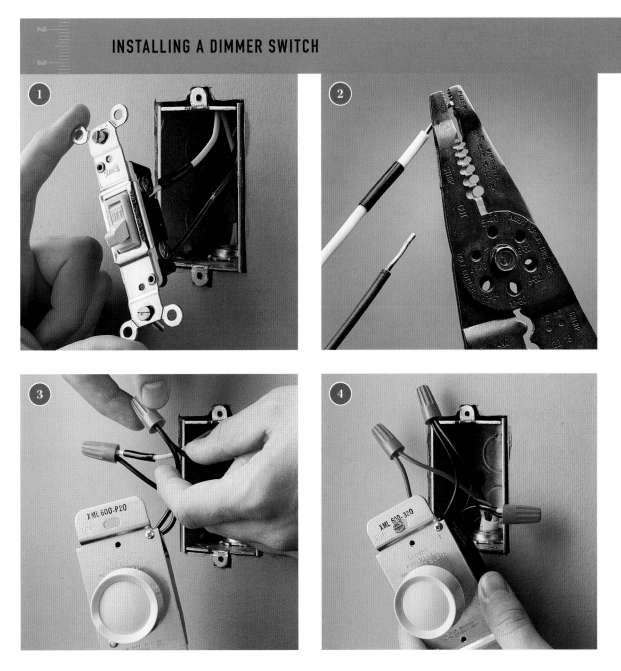

1   Turn off the power to the switch at the main service panel, then remove the cover plate and mounting screws. Holding the mounting straps carefully, pull the switch from the box. Be careful not to touch bare wires or screw terminals until they have been tested for power.

2   Disconnect the circuit wires and remove the switch. Straighten the circuit wires, and clip the ends, leaving about ½" of the bare wire end exposed.

3   Connect the wire leads on the dimmer switch to the circuit wires using wire connectors. The switch leads are interchangeable and can be attached to either of the two circuit wires.

4   A three-way dimmer has an additional wire lead. This "common" lead is connected to the common circuit wire. When replacing a standard three-way switch with a dimmer, the common circuit wire is attached to the darkest screw terminal on the old switch.

TESTING SWITCHES

A switch that does not work properly may have worn or broken internal parts. Test switches with a battery-operated continuity tester. The continuity tester detects any break in the metal pathway inside the switch. Replace the switch if the continuity tester shows the switch to be faulty.

Never use a continuity tester on wires that might carry live current. Always shut off the power and disconnect the switch before testing for continuity.

Some specialty switches, like dimmers, cannot be tested for continuity. Electronic switches can be tested for manual operation using a continuity tester, but the automatic operation of these switches cannot be tested.

TESTING A SINGLE-POLE WALL SWITCH

Clip

Probe

Low-voltage bulb

A   Attach the clip of the tester to one of the screw terminals. Touch the tester probe to the other screw terminal. Flip the switch lever from ON to OFF. If the switch is good, the tester glows when lever is ON, but not when OFF.

B   A continuity tester uses battery-generated current to test the metal pathways running through switches and other electrical fixtures. Always "test" the tester before use. Touch the tester clip to the metal probe. The tester should glow. If not, then the battery or lightbulb is dead and must be replaced.

TESTING A THREE-WAY WALL SWITCH

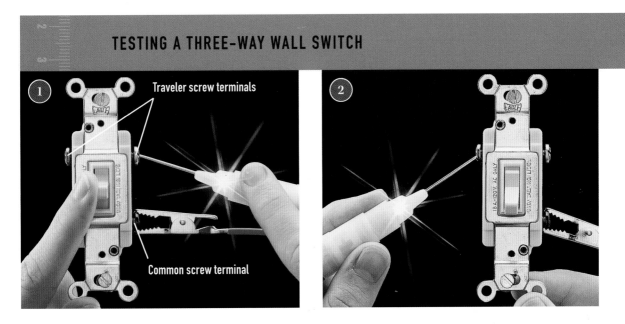

1   Attach the tester clip to the dark common screw terminal. Touch the tester probe to one of the traveler screw terminals, and flip the switch lever back and forth. If the switch is good, the tester should glow when the lever is in one position, but not both.

2   Touch the probe to the other traveler screw terminal, and flip the switch lever back and forth. If the switch is good, the tester will glow only when the switch lever is in the position opposite from the positive test in step 1.

TESTING A FOUR-WAY WALL SWITCH

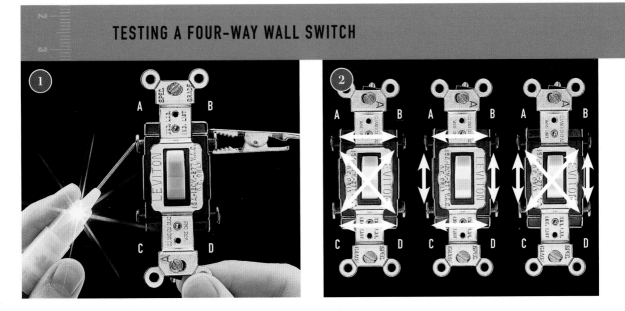

1   Test the switch by touching the probe and clip of the continuity tester to each pair of screw terminals (A-B, C-D, A-D, B-C, A-C, B-D). The test should show continuous pathways between two different pairs of screw terminals. Flip the lever to the opposite position, and repeat the test. The test should show continuous pathways between two different pairs of screw terminals.

2   If the switch is good, the test will show a total of four continuous pathways between screw terminals—two pathways for each lever position. If not, then the switch is faulty and must be replaced. (The arrangement of the pathways may differ, depending on the switch manufacturer. The photo above shows the three possible pathway arrangements.)

TESTING A PILOT-LIGHT SWITCH

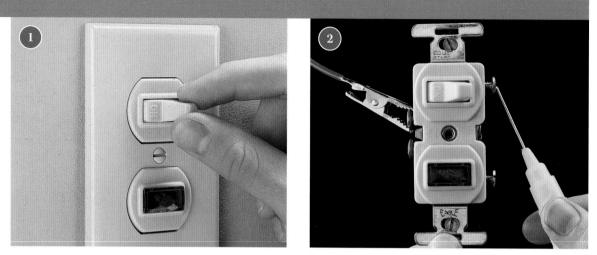

1   Test a pilot light by flipping the switch lever to the ON position. Check to see if the light fixture or appliance is working. If the pilot light does not glow even though the switch operates the light fixture or appliance, then the pilot light is defective and the unit must be replaced.

2   Test the switch by disconnecting the unit. With the switch lever in the ON position, attach the tester clip to the top screw terminal on one side of the switch. Touch the tester probe to top screw terminal on the opposite side of the switch. If the switch is good, the tester will glow when switch is ON, but not when OFF.

TESTING A TIMER SWITCH

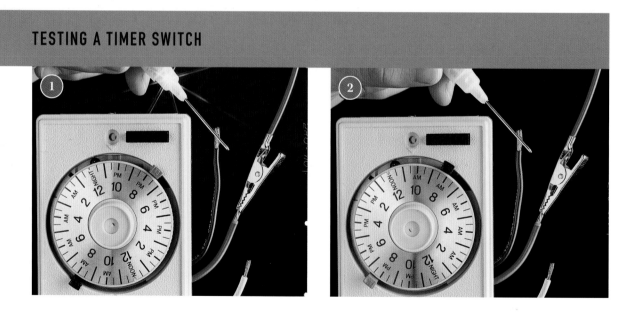

1   Attach the tester clip to the red wire lead on the timer switch, and touch the tester probe to the black hot lead. Rotate the timer dial clockwise until the ON tab passes the arrow marker. The tester should glow. If it does not, the switch is faulty and must be replaced.

2   Rotate the dial clockwise until the OFF tab passes the arrow marker. The tester should not glow. If it does, the switch is faulty and must be replaced.

TESTING A: A—SWITCH/RECEPTACLE, B—DOUBLE SWITCH, & C—TIME-DELAY SWITCH

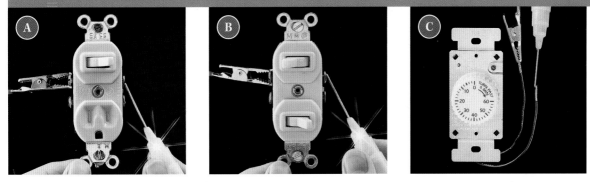

A   Attach the tester clip to one of the top screw terminals. Touch the tester probe to the top screw terminal on the opposite side. Flip the switch lever from ON to OFF position. If the switch is working correctly, the tester will glow when the switch lever is ON, but not when OFF.

B   Test each half of the switch by attaching the tester clip to one screw terminal and touching the probe to the opposite side. Flip the switch lever from ON to OFF position. If the switch is good, the tester glows when the switch lever is ON, but not when OFF. Repeat the test with the remaining pair of screw terminals. If either half tests faulty, replace the unit.

C   Attach the tester clip to one of the wire leads, and touch the tester probe to the other lead. Set the timer for a few minutes. If the switch is working correctly, the tester will glow until the time expires.

TESTING MANUAL OPERATION OF ELECTRONIC SWITCHES

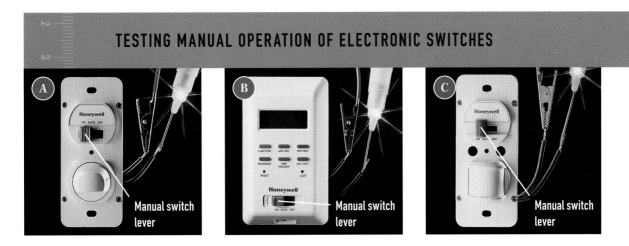

A   Automatic switch: Attach the tester clip to a black wire lead, and touch the tester probe to the other black lead. Flip the manual switch lever from ON to OFF position. If the switch is working correctly, the tester will glow when the switch lever is ON, but not when OFF.

B   Programmable switch: Attach the tester clip to a wire lead, and touch the tester probe to the other lead. Flip the manual switch lever from ON to OFF position. If the switch is working correctly, the tester will glow when the switch lever is ON, but not when OFF.

C   Motion-sensor switch: Attach the tester clip to a wire lead, and touch the tester probe to the other lead. Flip the manual switch lever from ON to OFF position. If the switch is working correctly, the tester will glow when the switch lever is ON, but not when OFF.

RECEPTACLE WIRING

A 120-volt duplex receptacle can be wired to the electrical system in a number of ways. The most common are shown on these pages.

Wiring configurations may vary slightly from these photographs, depending on the kind of receptacles used, the type of cable, or the technique of the electrician who installed the wiring. To make dependable repairs or replacements, use masking tape and label each wire according to its location on the terminals of the existing receptacle.

Receptacles are wired as either end-of-run or middle-of-run. These two basic configurations are easily identified by counting the number of cables entering the receptacle box. End-of-run wiring has only one cable, indicating that the circuit ends. Middle-of-run wiring has two cables, indicating that the circuit continues on to other receptacles, switches, or fixtures.

A split-circuit receptacle is shown on the next page. Each half of a split-circuit receptacle is wired to a separate circuit. This allows two appliances of high wattage to be plugged into the same receptacle without blowing a fuse or tripping a breaker. This wiring configuration is similar to a receptacle that is controlled by a wall switch. Code requires a switch-controlled receptacle in any room that does not have a built-in light fixture operated by a wall switch.

Split-circuit and switch-controlled receptacles are connected to two hot wires, so use caution during repairs or replacements. Make sure the connecting tab between the hot screw terminals is removed.

Two-slot receptacles are common in older homes. There is no grounding wire attached to the receptacle, but the box may be grounded with armored cable or conduit. Tamper-resistant receptacles are now required in all new residential installations.

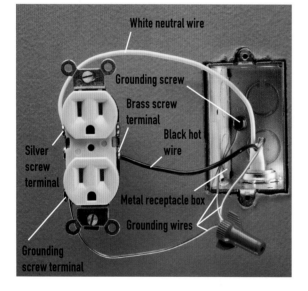

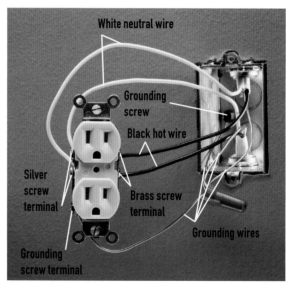

Single cable entering the box indicates end-of-run wiring. The black hot wire is attached to a brass screw terminal, and the white neutral wire is connected to a silver screw terminal. If the box is metal, the grounding wire is pigtailed to the grounding screws of the receptacle and the box. In a plastic box, the grounding wire is attached directly to the grounding screw terminal of the receptacle.

Two cables entering the box indicate middle-of-run wiring. Black hot wires are connected to brass screw terminals, and white neutral wires to silver screw terminals. The grounding wire is pigtailed to the grounding screws of the receptacle and the box.

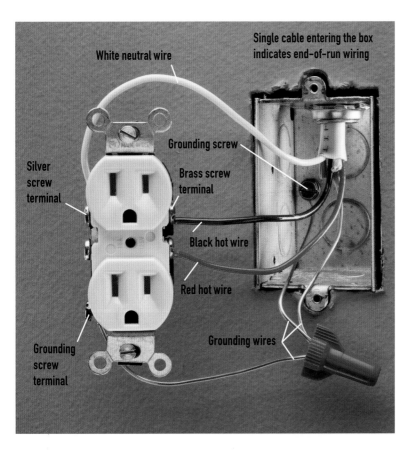

White neutral wire

Single cable entering the box indicates end-of-run wiring

Grounding screw

Silver screw terminal

Brass screw terminal

Black hot wire

Red hot wire

Grounding wires

Grounding screw terminal

A split-circuit receptacle is attached to a black hot wire, a red hot wire, a white neutral wire, and a bare grounding wire. The wiring is similar to a switch-controlled receptacle. The hot wires are attached to the brass screw terminals, and the connecting tab or fin between the brass terminals is removed. The white wire is attached to a silver screw terminal, and the connecting tab on the neutral side remains intact. The grounding wire is pigtailed to the grounding screw terminal of the receptacle and to the grounding screw attached to the box.

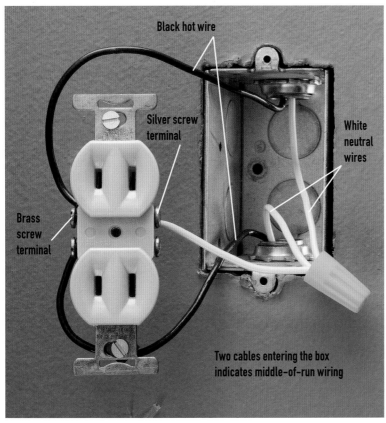

Black hot wire

Silver screw terminal

White neutral wires

Brass screw terminal

Two cables entering the box indicates middle-of-run wiring

A two-slot receptacle is often found in older homes. The black hot wires are connected to the brass screw terminals, and the white neutral wires are pigtailed to a silver screw terminal. Two-slot receptacles may be replaced with three-slot types, but only if a means of grounding exists at the receptacle box. In some municipalities, you may replace a two-slot receptacle with a GFCI receptacle as long as the receptacle has a sticker that reads "No equipment ground."

Duplex Receptacles

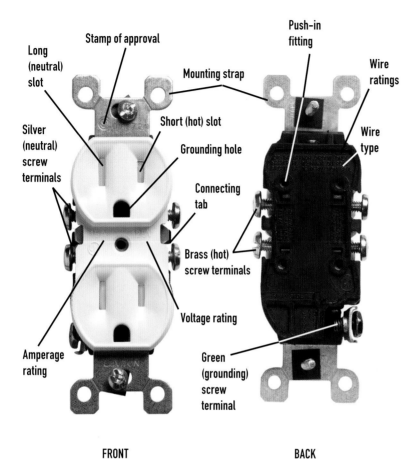

Long (neutral) slot

Stamp of approval

Mounting strap

Silver (neutral) screw terminals

Short (hot) slot

Grounding hole

Connecting tab

Brass (hot) screw terminals

Amperage rating

Voltage rating

Push-in fitting

Wire ratings

Wire type

Green (grounding) screw terminal

FRONT

BACK

The polarized receptacle
became standard in the 1920s. The different sized slots direct current flow for safety.

The standard duplex receptacle has two halves for receiving plugs. Each half has a long (neutral) slot, a short (hot) slot, and a U-shaped grounding hole. The slots fit the wide prong, narrow prong, and grounding prong of a three-prong plug. This ensures that the connection between receptacle and plug will be polarized and grounded for safety.

Wires are attached to the receptacle at screw terminals or push-in fittings. A connecting tab between the screw terminals allows a variety of different wiring configurations. Receptacles also include mounting straps for attaching to electrical boxes.

Stamps of approval from testing agencies are found on the front and back of the receptacle. Look for the symbol UL or UND LAB INC LIST to make sure the receptacle meets the strict standards of Underwriters Laboratories.

The receptacle is marked with ratings for maximum volts and amps. The common receptacle is marked 15A, 125V. Receptacles marked CU or COPPER are used with solid copper wire. Those marked CU-CLAD ONLY are used with copper-coated aluminum wire. Only receptacles marked CO/ALR may be used with solid aluminum wiring. Receptacles marked AL/CU no longer may be used with aluminum wire, according to code.

The ground-fault circuit-interrupter,
or GFCI receptacle, is a modern safety device. When it detects slight changes in current, it instantly shuts off power.

Common Receptacle Problems

Household receptacles, also called outlets, have no moving parts to wear out and usually last for many years without servicing. Most problems associated with receptacles are actually caused by faulty lamps and appliances, or their plugs and cords. However, the constant plugging in and removal of appliance cords can wear out the metal contacts inside a receptacle. Any receptacle that does not hold plugs firmly should be replaced. In addition, older receptacles made of hard plastic may harden and crack with age. They must be replaced when this happens.

A loose wire connection with the receptacle box is another possible problem. A loose connection can spark (called arcing), trip a circuit breaker, or cause heat to build up in the receptacle box, creating a potential fire hazard.

Wires can come loose for a number of reasons. Everyday vibrations caused by walking across floors, or from nearby street traffic, may cause a connection to shake loose. In addition, because wires heat and cool with normal use, the ends of the wires will expand and contract slightly. This movement also may cause the wires to come loose from the screw terminal connections.

Not all receptacles are created equally. When replacing, make sure to buy one with the same amp rating as the old one. Inadvertently installing a 20-amp receptacle in replacement of a 15-amp receptacle is a very common error.

Problem	Repair
Circuit breaker trips repeatedly, or fuse burns out immediately after being replaced.	1. Repair or replace worn or damaged lamp or appliance cord. 2. Move lamps or appliances to other circuits to prevent overloads. 3. Tighten any loose wire connections. 4. Clean dirty or oxidized wire ends.
Lamp or appliance does not work.	1. Make sure lamp or appliance is plugged in. 2. Replace burned–out bulbs. 3. Repair or replace worn or damaged lamp or appliance cord. 4. Tighten any loose wire connections. 5. Clean dirty or oxidized wire ends. 6. Repair or replace any faulty receptacle.
Receptacle does not hold plugs firmly.	1. Repair or replace worn or damaged plugs. 2. Replace faulty receptacle.
Receptacle is warm to the touch, buzzes, or sparks when plugs are inserted or removed.	1. Move lamps or appliances to other circuits to prevent overloads. 2. Tighten any loose wire connections. 3. Clean dirty or oxidized wire ends. 4. Replace faulty receptacle.

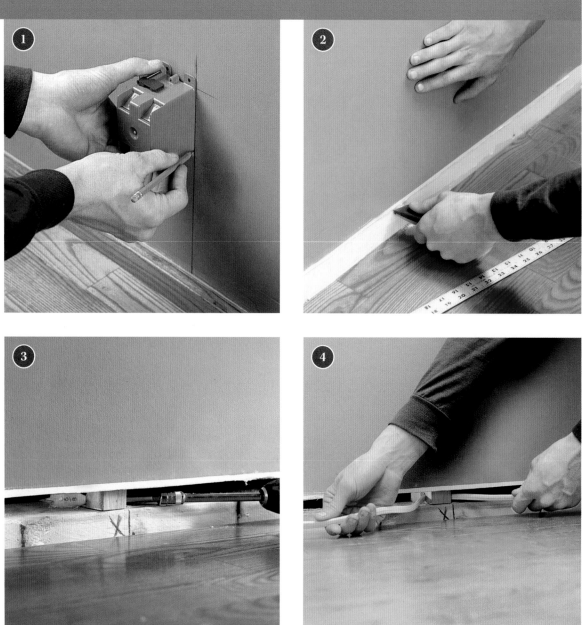

1   Position the new pop-in box on the wall and trace around it. Consider the location of hidden utilities within the wall before you cut.

2   Remove baseboard between the new and existing receptacle. Cut away the drywall about 1" below the baseboard with a jigsaw, wallboard saw, or utility knife.

3   Drill a ⅝" hole in the center of each stud along the opening between the two receptacles. A drill bit extender or a flexible drill bit will allow you a better angle and make drilling the holes easier.

4   Run the branch cable through the holes from the new location to the existing receptacle. Staple the cable to the stud below the box. Install a metal nail plate on the front edge of each stud that the cable routes through.

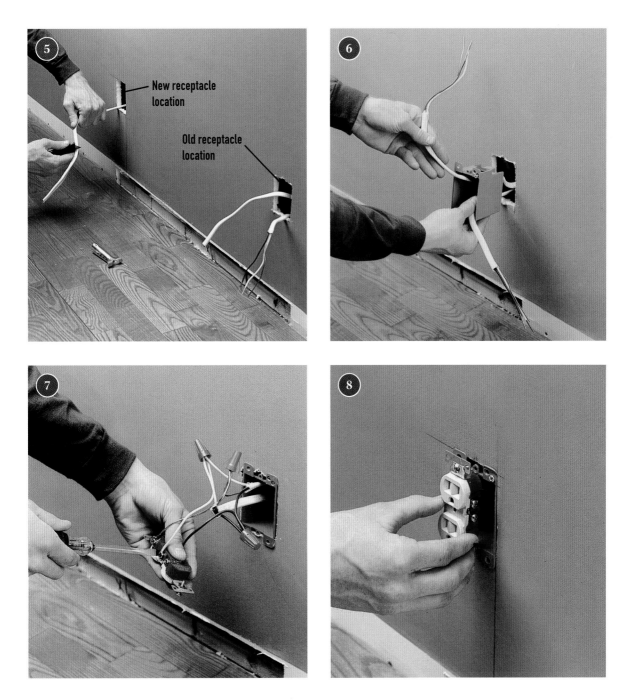

New receptacle location

Old receptacle location

5   Turn off the power at the main panel and test for power. Remove the old receptacle and its box, and pull the new branch cable up through the hole. Remove sheathing and insulation from both ends of the new cable.

6   Thread the new and old cables into a pop-in box large enough to contain the added wires and clamp the cables. Fit the box into the old hole and attach it.

7   Reconnect the old receptacle by connecting its neutral, hot, and grounding screws to the new branch cable and the old cable from the panel with pigtails.

8   Pull the cable through another pop-in box for the new receptacle. Secure the cable and install the box. Connect the new receptacle to the new branch cable. Insert the receptacle into the box and attach the receptacle and cover plate with screws. Patch the opening with ½"-thick wood strips or drywall. Reattach the baseboard to the studs.

GFCI RECEPTACLES

The ground-fault circuit-interrupter (GFCI) receptacle protects against electrical shock caused by a faulty appliance, or a worn cord or plug. It senses small changes in current flow and can shut off power in as little as $\frac{1}{40}$ of a second.

GFCIs are now required in bathrooms, kitchens, garages, crawl spaces, unfinished basements, and outdoor receptacle locations. Consult your local codes for any requirements regarding the installation of GFCI receptacles. Most GFCIs use standard screw terminal connections, but some have wire leads and are attached with wire connectors. Because the body of a GFCI receptacle is larger than a standard receptacle, small crowded electrical boxes may need to be replaced with more spacious boxes.

The GFCI receptacle may be wired to protect only itself (single location), or it can be wired to protect all receptacles, switches, and light fixtures from the GFCI "forward" to the end of the circuit (multiple locations).

Because the GFCI is so sensitive, it is most effective when wired to protect a single location. The more receptacles any one GFCI protects, the more susceptible it is to "phantom tripping," shutting off power because of tiny, normal fluctuations in current flow. GFCI receptacles installed in outdoor locations must be rated for outdoor use and weather resistance (WR) along with ground fault protection.

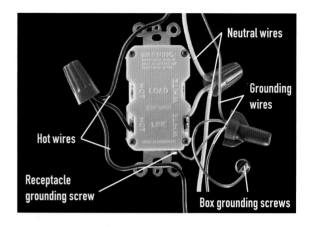

A GFCI wired for single-location protection (shown from the back) has hot and neutral wires connected only to the screw terminals marked LINE. A GFCI connected for single-location protection may be wired as either an end-of-run or middle-of-run configuration.

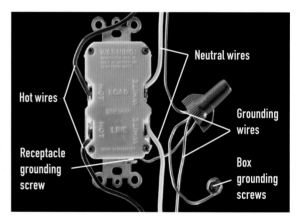

A GFCI wired for multiple-location protection (shown from the back) has one set of hot and neutral wires connected to the LINE pair of screw terminals, and the other set connected to the LOAD pair of screw terminals. A GFCI receptacle connected for multiple-location protection may be wired only as a middle-of-run configuration.

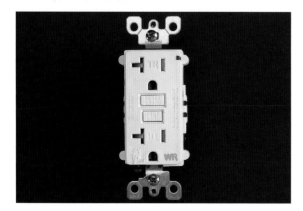

Modern GFCI receptacles have tamper-resistant slots. Look for a model that's rated "WR" (for weather resistance) if you'll be installing it outdoors or in a wet location.

Tools & Materials

Circuit tester

Screwdriver

Wire connectors

Masking tape

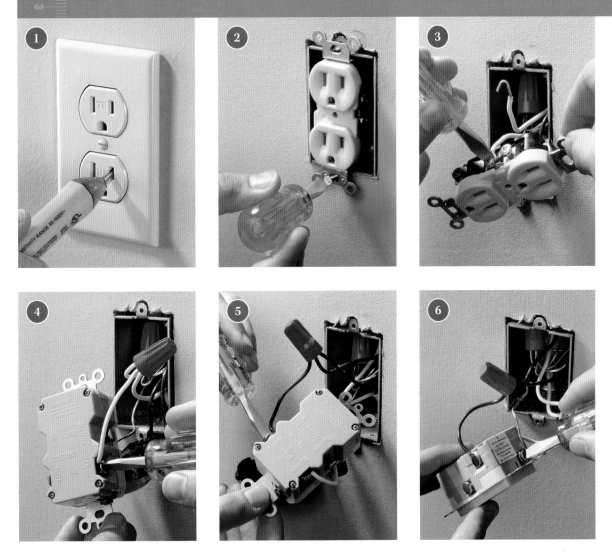

1   Shut off power to the receptacle at the main service panel. Test for power with a neon circuit tester. Be sure to check both halves of the receptacle.

2   Remove cover plate. Loosen mounting screws, and gently pull receptacle from the box. Do not touch wires. Confirm power is off with a circuit tester.

3   Disconnect all white neutral wires from the silver screw terminals of the old receptacle.

4   Pigtail all the white neutral wires together, and connect the pigtail to the terminal marked WHITE LINE on the GFCI (see photo on opposite page).

5   Disconnect all black hot wires from the brass screw terminals of the old receptacle. Pigtail these wires together, and connect them to the terminal marked HOT LINE on the GFCI.

6   If a grounding wire is available, connect it to the green grounding screw terminal of the GFCI. Mount the GFCI in the receptacle box, and reattach the cover plate. Restore power, and test the GFCI according to the manufacturer's instructions.

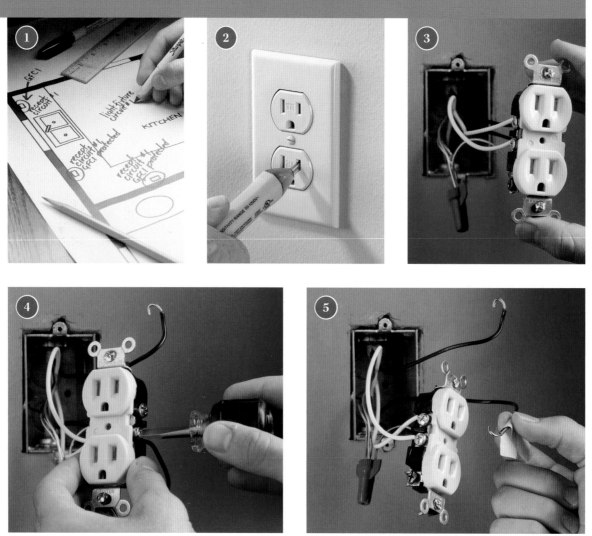

1   Use a map of your house circuits to determine a location for your GFCI. Indicate all receptacles that will be protected by the GFCI installation.

2   Turn off power to the correct circuit at the main service panel. Test all the receptacles in the circuit with a neon circuit tester to make sure the power is off. Always check both halves of each duplex receptacle.

3   Remove the cover plate from the receptacle that will be replaced with the GFCI. Loosen the mounting screws and gently pull the receptacle from its box. Take care not to touch any bare wires. Confirm the power is off with a neon circuit tester.

4   Disconnect all black hot wires. Carefully separate the hot wires and position them so that the bare ends do not touch anything. Restore power to the circuit at the main service panel. Determine which black wire is the feed wire by testing for hot wires. The feed wire brings power to the receptacle from the service panel. Use caution: This is a live wire test, during which the power is turned on temporarily.

5   When you have found the hot feed wire, turn off power at the main service panel. Identify the feed wire by marking it with masking tape.

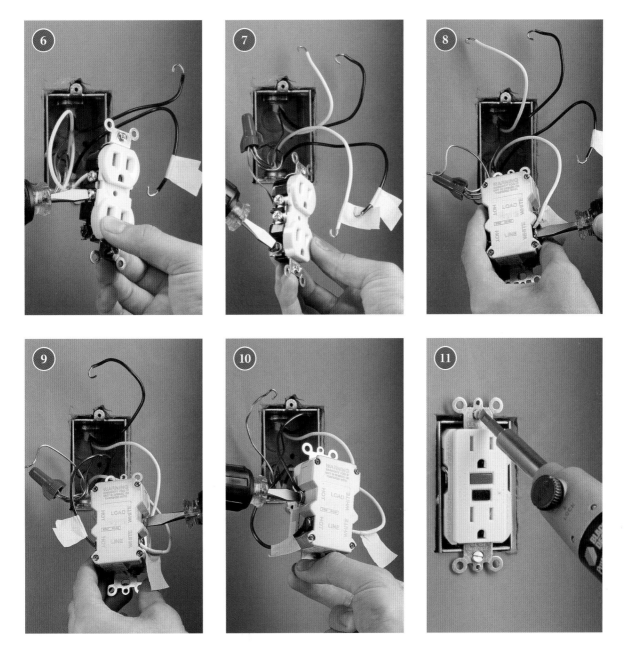

6   Disconnect the white neutral wires from the old receptacle. Identify the white feed wire and label it with masking tape. The white feed wire will be the one that shares the same cable as the black feed wire.

7   Disconnect the grounding wire from the grounding screw terminal of the old receptacle. Remove the old receptacle. Connect the grounding wire to the grounding screw terminal of the GFCI.

8   Connect the white feed wire to the terminal marked WHITE LINE on the GFCI. Connect the black feed wire to the terminal marked HOT LINE on the GFCI.

9   Connect the other white neutral wire to the terminal marked WHITE LOAD on the GFCI.

10   Connect the other black hot wire to the terminal marked HOT LOAD on the GFCI.

11   Carefully tuck all wires into the receptacle box. Mount the GFCI in the box and attach the cover plate. Turn on power to the circuit at the main service panel. Test the GFCI according to the manufacturer's instructions.

TESTING RECEPTACLES

For testing receptacles and other devices for power, grounding, and polarity, neon circuit testers are inexpensive and easy to use. But they are less sensitive than auto-ranging multimeters. In some cases, neon testers won't detect the presence of lower voltage in a circuit. This can lead you to believe that a circuit is shut off when it is not—a dangerous mistake. The small probes on a neon circuit tester also force you to get too close to live terminals and wires. For a quick check and confirmation, a neon circuit tester (or a plug-in tester) is adequate. But for the most reliable readings, buy and learn to use a multimeter.

The best multimeters are auto-ranging models with a digital readout. Unlike manual multimeters, auto-ranging models do not require you to preset the voltage range to get an accurate reading. Unlike neon testers, multimeters may be used for a host of additional diagnostic functions such as testing fuses, measuring battery voltage, testing internal wiring in appliances, and checking light fixtures to determine if they're functional.

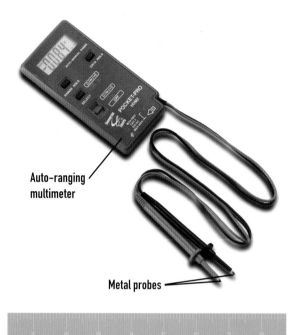

Auto-ranging multimeter

Metal probes

Tools & Materials

Multimeter

Touchless circuit tester

Plug-in tester

Screwdriver

USING A PLUG-IN TESTER

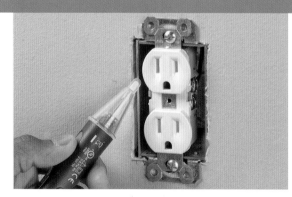

Use a touchless circuit tester to verify that power is not flowing to a receptacle. Using either a no-touch sensor or a probe-style circuit tester, test the receptacle for current before you remove the cover plate. Once the plate is removed, double-check at the terminals to make sure there is no current.

TESTING QUICKLY FOR POWER

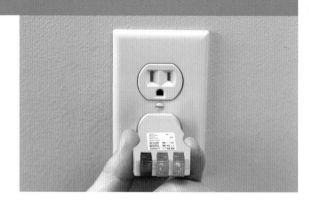

Use a plug-in tester to test a three-slot receptacle. With the power on, insert the tester into the suspect outlet. The face of the tester has three colored lights that will light up in different combinations, according to the outlet's problem. A reference chart is provided with the tester, and may have a chart on the tester itself.

1   Set the selector dial for alternating-current voltage. Plug the black probe lead into the common jack on the multimeter (labeled COM). Plug the red probe lead into the V-labeled jack.

2   Insert the test ends of the probe into the receptacle slots. It does not make a difference which probe goes into which slot as long as they're in the same receptacle. If power is present and flowing normally, you will see a voltage reading on the readout screen.

3   If the multimeter reads 0 or gives a very low reading (less than 1 or 2 volts), power is not present in the receptacle and it is safe to remove the cover plate and work on the fixture (although it's always a good idea to confirm your reading by touching the probes directly to the screw terminals on the receptacles).

Option:

When a receptacle or switch is in the middle of a circuit, it is difficult to tell which wires are carrying current. Use a multimeter to check. With power off, remove the receptacle and separate the wires. Restore power. Touch one probe to the bare ground or the grounded metal box and touch the other probe to the end of each wire. The wire that shows current on the meter is hot.

WIRING PROJECTS

EVEN THOUGH THIS BOOK does not cover a major wiring construction project in detail, here are some guidelines for a major project, should you decide to pursue one.

Careful planning of a wiring project ensures you will have plenty of power for present and future needs. Whether you are adding circuits in a room addition, wiring a remodeled kitchen, or adding an outdoor circuit, consider all possible ways the space might be used, and plan for enough electrical service to meet peak needs.

A large wiring project adds a considerable load to your main electrical service. In about 25 percent of all homes, some type of service upgrade is needed before new wiring can be installed. This chapter gives an easy five-step method for determining your electrical needs and planning new circuits.

Five Steps for Planning a Wiring Project

1   Examine your main service panel. The amp rating of the electrical service and the size of the circuit breaker panel will help you determine if a service upgrade is needed.

2   Learn about codes. The National Electrical Code (NEC), and local electrical codes and building codes, provide guidelines for determining how much power and how many circuits your home needs. Your local electrical inspector can tell you which regulations apply to your job.

3   Prepare for inspections. Remember that your work must be reviewed by your local electrical inspector. When planning your wiring project, always follow the inspector's guidelines for quality workmanship.

4   Evaluate electrical loads. New circuits put an added load on your electrical service. Make sure that the total load of the existing wiring and the planned new circuits does not exceed the main service capacity.

5   Draw a wiring diagram and get a permit. This wiring plan will help you organize your work.

Examine Your Main Service Panel

The first step in planning a new wiring project is to look in your main circuit breaker panel and find the size of the service by reading the amperage rating on the main circuit breaker. As you plan new circuits and evaluate electrical loads, knowing the size of the main service helps you determine if you need a service upgrade.

Also look for open circuit breaker slots in the panel. The number of open slots will determine if you need to add a circuit breaker subpanel.

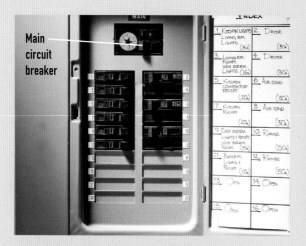

Find the service size by opening the main service panel and reading the amp rating printed on the main circuit breaker. In most cases, 100-amp service provides enough power to handle the added loads of projects like the ones shown in this book. A service rated for 60 amps or less may need to be upgraded.

Older service panels use fuses instead of circuit breakers. Have an electrician replace this type of panel with a circuit breaker panel that provides enough power and enough open breaker slots for the new circuits you are planning.

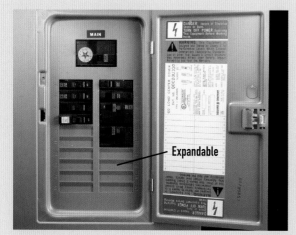

Look for open circuit breaker slots in the main circuit breaker panel or in a circuit breaker subpanel, if your home already has one. You will need one open slot for each 120-volt circuit you plan to install and two slots for each 240-volt circuit. If your main circuit breaker panel has no open breaker slots, install a subpanel to provide room for connecting new circuits.

Learn About Codes

To ensure public safety, your community requires that you get a permit to install new wiring and have the completed work reviewed by an appointed inspector. Electrical inspectors use the National Electrical Code (NEC) as the primary authority for evaluating wiring, but they also follow the local Building Code and Electrical Code standards.

As you begin planning new circuits, call or visit your local electrical inspector and discuss the project with him. The inspector can tell you which of the national and local code requirements apply to your job, and may give you a packet of information summarizing these regulations. Later, when you apply to the inspector for a work permit, he will expect you to understand the local guidelines as well as a few basic National Electrical Code requirements.

The National Electrical Code is a set of standards that provides minimum safety requirements for wiring installations. It is revised every three years. The national code requirements for the projects shown in this book are thoroughly explained on the following pages. For more information, you can find copies of the current NEC, as well as a number of excellent handbooks based on the NEC, at libraries and bookstores.

In addition to being the final authority of code requirements, inspectors are electrical professionals with years of experience. Although they have busy schedules, most inspectors are happy to answer questions and help you design well-planned circuits.

Basic Electrical Code Requirements

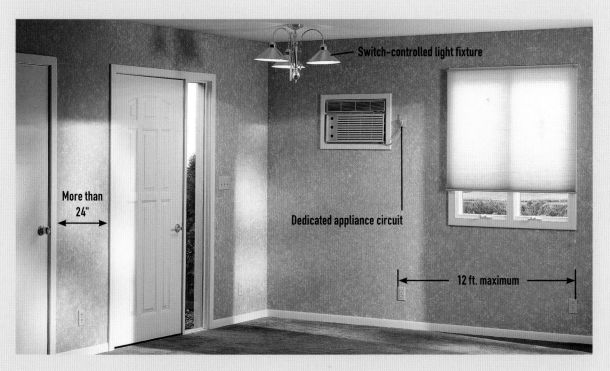

Electrical Code requirements for living areas: Living areas need at least one 15-amp or 20-amp basic lighting/receptacle circuit for each 600 sq. ft. of living space and should have a dedicated circuit for each type of permanent appliance, like an air conditioner, computer, or a group of baseboard heaters and within 6 ft. of any door opening. Receptacles on basic lighting/receptacle circuits should be spaced no more than 12 ft. apart. Many electricians and electrical inspectors recommend even closer spacing. Any wall more than 24" wide also needs a receptacle. Every room should have a wall switch at the point of entry to control either a ceiling light or plug-in lamp. Kitchens and bathrooms must have a ceiling-mounted light fixture.

Three-way switches

Measure the living areas of your home, excluding closets and unfinished spaces. A sonic measuring tool gives room dimensions quickly and contains a built-in calculator for figuring floor area. You will need a minimum of one basic lighting/receptacle circuit for every 600 sq. ft. of living space. The total square footage also helps you determine heating and cooling needs for new room additions.

Stairways with six steps or more must have lighting that illuminates each step. The light fixture must be controlled by three-way switches at the top and bottom landings.

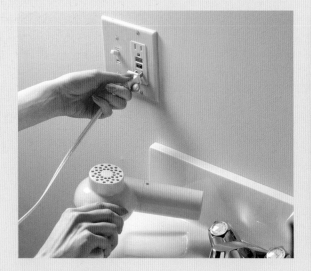

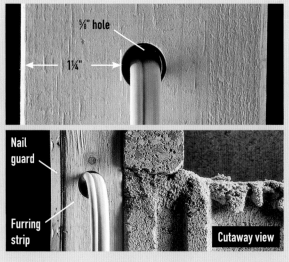

⅝" hole

1¼"

Nail guard

Furring strip

Cutaway view

Kitchen and bathroom receptacles must be protected by a ground-fault circuit-interrupter (GFCI). Also, all outdoor receptacles and general-use receptacles in an unfinished basement or crawl space and garages must be protected by a GFCI.

Cables must be protected against damage from nails and screws by at least 1¼" of wood (top). When cables pass through 2 × 2 furring strips (bottom), protect the cables with metal nail guards. Nail guards also may be used to protect cable that cannot meet the 1¼" of wood protection standard.

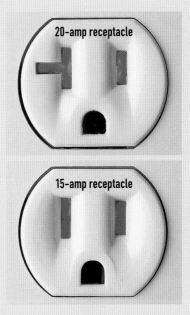

Closets and other storage spaces need at least one light fixture that is controlled by a wall switch near the entrance. Prevent fire hazards by positioning the light fixtures so the outer globes are at least 12" away from all shelf areas.

Hallways more than 10 ft. long need at least one receptacle. All hallways should have a switch-controlled light fixture.

Amp ratings of receptacles must match the size of the circuit. A common mistake is to use 20-amp receptacles (top) on 15-amp circuits—a potential cause of dangerous circuit overloads because it allows you to plug in appliances that draw over 15 amps.

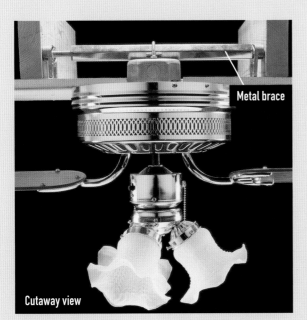
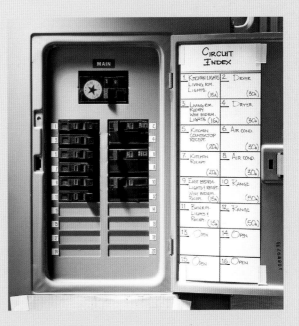

A metal brace attached to framing members is required for ceiling fans and large light fixtures that are too heavy to be supported by an electrical box. All ceiling fans must be installed in a box that is fan-rated.

Label new circuits on an index attached to the circuit breaker panel. List the rooms and appliances controlled by each circuit. Make sure the area around the panel is clean, well lighted, and accessible.

GFCI & AFCI Breakers

Tools & Materials
Insulated screwdriver
Circuit tester
Combination tool
AFCI or GFCI breaker

AFCI breakers (right) are similar in appearance to GFCI breakers (left), but they function differently. AFCI breakers trip when they sense an arc fault. GFCI breakers trip when they sense fault between the hot wire and the ground.

UNDERSTANDING THE DIFFERENCE between GFCI (ground-fault circuit interruption) and AFCI (arc fault circuit interruption) is very tricky for most homeowners who do not have a degree in electrical engineering. Essentially, it comes down to this: Arc-fault protection keeps your house from burning down; ground-fault protection keeps people from being electrocuted.

The National Electric Code (NEC) requires that an arc-fault circuit-interrupter (AFCI) breaker be installed on all branch circuits that supply outlets or fixtures in newly constructed homes. They're a prudent precaution in any home, especially if it has older wiring. AFCI breakers will not interfere with the operation of GFCI receptacles, so it is safe to install an AFCI breaker on a circuit that contains GFCI receptacles.

A GFCI breaker is an important safety device that disconnects a circuit in the event of a ground fault (when current takes a path other than the neutral back to the panel).

On new construction, GFCI protection is required on outlets in laundry and utility rooms, garages and unfinished basements, and near kitchen or bathroom sinks. In general it is a good practice to protect all receptacle and fixture locations that could encounter damp or wet circumstances. Typically, a GFCI receptacle is installed at each location, but in some cases—outdoor circuits or older homes with boxes too shallow for GFCI receptacles, for instance—it is advisable to protect the entire circuit with a GFCI breaker.

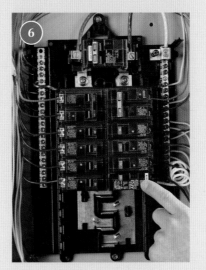

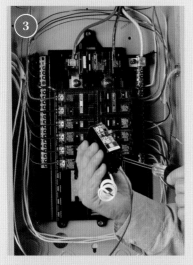

1   Locate the breaker for the circuit you'd like to protect. Then turn off the main circuit breaker. Remove the cover from the panel, and test to ensure that power is off. Remove the breaker you want to replace from the panel. Remove the black wire from the LOAD terminal of the breaker.

2   Find the white wire on the circuit you want to protect, and remove it from the neutral bus bar.

3   Flip the handle of the new AFCI or GFCI breaker to OFF. Loosen both of the breaker's terminal screws. Connect the white circuit wire to the breaker terminal labeled PANEL NEUTRAL. Connect the black circuit wire to the breaker terminal labeled LOAD POWER.

4   Connect the new breaker's coiled white wire to the neutral bus bar on the service panel.

5   Make sure all the connections are tight. Snap the new breaker into the bus bar.

6   Turn the main breaker on. Turn off and unplug all fixtures and appliances on the AFCI or GFCI breaker circuit. Turn the AFCI or GFCI breaker on. Press the test button. If the breaker is wired correctly, the breaker trips open. If it doesn't trip, check all connections or consult an electrician. Replace the panel cover.

120/240-Volt Dryer Receptacles

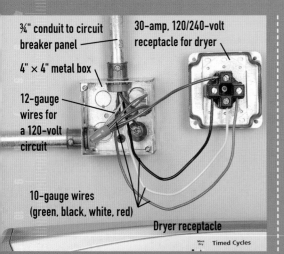

¾" conduit to circuit breaker panel

30-amp, 120/240-volt receptacle for dryer

4" × 4" metal box

12-gauge wires for a 120-volt circuit

10-gauge wires (green, black, white, red)

Dryer receptacle

Timed Cycles

Tools & Materials

Combination tool
Drill
Circuit tester
Hammer
Screwdriver
30-amp double-pole breaker

30-amp 120/240-volt dryer receptacle
10/3 NM cable or 10-gauge THHN/THWN
Receptacle box
Conduit (for masonry walls)

A 240-volt installation is no more complicated than wiring a single-pole breaker and outlet. The main difference is that the dryer circuit's double-pole breaker is designed to contact both 120-volt bus bars in the service panel. Together, these two 120-volt circuits serve the dryer's heating elements with 240 volts of power. The timer, switches, and other dryer electronics utilize the circuit's 120-volt power.

MANY DRYERS require both 120- and 240-volt power. If you are installing this type of electric dryer, you will need to install a 30-amp, 120/240-volt receptacle that feeds from a dedicated 30-amp double-pole breaker in your service panel. Verify your dryer's electric requirements before wiring a new receptacle.

Begin the installation by identifying a location for the dryer receptacle. Run 10/3 NM cable from the service panel to the new receptacle. If you are mounting the dryer receptacle box on an unfinished masonry wall, run the THNN wire in conduit and secure the box and conduit with masonry screws. If you are mounting the receptacle box in finished drywall, cut a hole, fish the cable through, and mount the receptacle in the wall opening.

INSTALLING A 120/240-VOLT DRYER RECEPTACLE

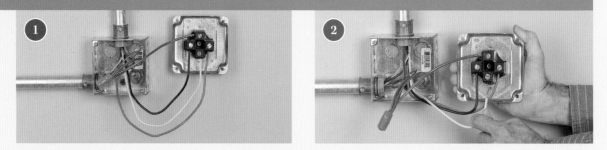

1   Connect the white neutral wire to the silver neutral screw terminal. Connect each of the black and the red wires to either of the brass screw terminals (the terminals are interchangeable). Connect the green ground wire to the receptacle grounding screw. Attach the cover plate.

2   With the service panel main breaker shut off, connect the dryer cable to a dedicated 30-amp double-pole breaker. Connect the ground wire to the panel grounding bar. Connect the white neutral wire to the neutral bar. Connect the red and the black wires to the two brass screw terminals on the breaker. Snap the breaker into the bus bar. Attach the panel cover. Turn the breakers on and test the circuit.

120/240-Volt Range Receptacles

MANY ELECTRIC RANGES require both 120- and 240-volt power. If you are installing this type of electric range, you will need to install a 40- or 50-amp 120/240-volt receptacle that feeds from a dedicated 40- or 50-amp breaker in the service panel. Breaker amperage depends on the amount of power the range draws. Verify requirements before wiring a receptacle.

A range receptacle and breaker installation is no more complicated than wiring a single-pole breaker and outlet. The main difference is that the range circuit's double-pole breaker is designed to contact both 120-volt bus bars in the service panel. Together these two 120-volt circuits serve the range's heating elements with 240 volts of power. The timer, switches, and other range electronics utilize the circuit's 120-volt power.

Modern range receptacles accept a four-prong plug configuration. The cable required is four-conductor service entrance round (SE or NM-B) cable, containing three insulated wires and one ground. The two hot wires might be black and red (shown below) or black and black with a red stripe. The neutral wire is generally white or gray. The grounding wire is green or bare. The size used for a kitchen range is usually 6/3 grounded SE or NM-B copper cable. The receptacle itself is generally surface mounted for easier installation (shown below), though flush-mounted units are also available.

Tools & Materials

Combination tool	Hammer	Surface-mounted range receptacle
Circuit tester	Screwdriver	6/3 grounded SER cable
Drill	Drywall saw	50- or 60-amp double-pole
	Fish tape	circuit breaker

INSTALLING A KITCHEN RANGE RECEPTACLE

1   Turn power off. Identify a location for the surface-mounted range receptacle. Cut a small hole in the wall. Fish the SER cable from the service panel into the wall opening. Thread the cable into a surface-mounted receptacle and clamp it. Strip insulation from the individual wires.

2   Wire the receptacle. Connect the bare copper ground wire to the receptacle grounding screw. Connect the white neutral wire to the silver neutral screw terminal. Connect each of the hot (black and red) wires to either of the brass screw terminals (the terminals are interchangeable). Mount the housing on the wall and attach the cover plate.

3   Wire the SER cable to a 40- or 50-amp breaker. With the main breaker off, remove the panel cover. Remove a knockout from the panel and feed the cable into the panel. Connect the ground wire to the grounding bar. Connect the neutral wire from the cable to the neutral bar. Connect the red and the black wires to the two brass screw terminals on the breaker. Snap it into the bus bar. Attach the panel cover. Turn the breakers on and test the circuit.

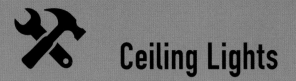

Ceiling Lights

Installing a new ceiling fixture can provide more light to a space, not to mention an aesthetic lift. It's one of the easiest upgrades you can do.

Tools & Materials

Replacement light fixture
Wire stripper
Voltage sensor
Insulated screwdrivers
Wire connectors
Eye protection

CEILING FIXTURES don't have any moving parts and their wiring is very simple, so, other than changing bulbs, you're likely to get decades of trouble-free service from a fixture. This sounds like a good thing, but it also means that the fixture probably won't fail and give you an excuse to update a room's look with a new one. Fortunately, you don't need an excuse. Upgrading a fixture is easy and can make a dramatic impact on a room. You can substantially increase the light in a room by replacing a globe-style fixture with one that has separate spot lights, or you can simply install a new fixture that matches the room's décor.

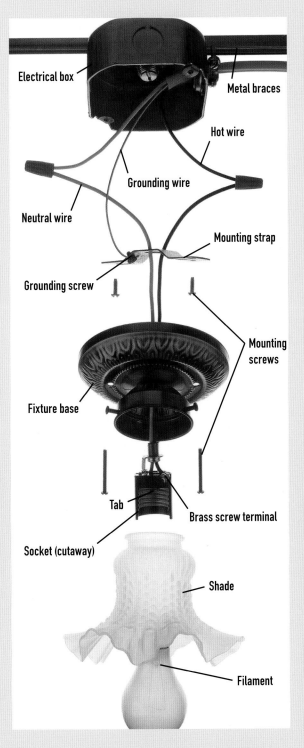

Electrical box

Metal braces

Hot wire

Grounding wire

Neutral wire

Mounting strap

Grounding screw

Mounting screws

Fixture base

Tab

Brass screw terminal

Socket (cutaway)

Shade

Filament

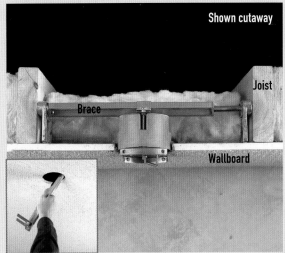

Shown cutaway

Joist

Brace

Wallboard

If the new fixture is much heavier than the original fixture, it will require additional bracing in the ceiling to support the electrical box and the fixture. The manufacturer's instructions should specify the size and type of box. If the ceiling is finished and there is no access from above, you can remove the old box and use an adjustable remodeling brace appropriate for your fixture (shown). The brace fits into a small hole in the ceiling (inset). Once the bracing is in place, install a new electrical box specified for the new fixture.

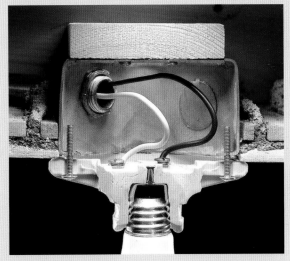

No matter what a ceiling light fixture looks like on the outside, they all attach in basically the same way. An electrical box in the ceiling is fitted with a mounting strap, which holds the fixture in place. The bare wire from the ceiling typically connects to the mounting strap. The two wires coming from the fixture connect to the black and the white wires from the ceiling.

Inexpensive light fixtures have screw terminals mounted directly to the backside of the fixture plate. Often, as Seen here, they have no grounding terminal. Some codes do not allow this type of fixture, but even if your hometown does approve them, it is a good idea to replace them with a better quality, safer fixture that is UL-approved.

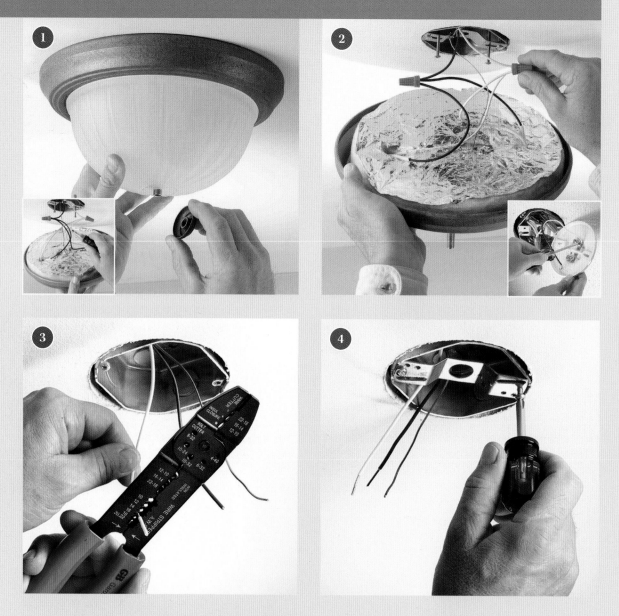

1   Shut off power to the ceiling light and remove the shade or diffuser. Loosen the mounting screws and carefully lower the fixture, supporting it as you work (do not let light fixtures hang by their electrical wires alone). Test with a voltage sensor to make sure no power is reaching the connections.

2   Remove the twist connectors from the fixture wires or unscrew the screw terminals and remove the white neutral wire and the black lead wire (inset).

3   Before you install the new fixture, check the ends of the wires coming from the ceiling electrical box. They should be clean and free of nicks or scorch marks. If they're dirty or worn, clip off the stripped portion with your combination tool. Then strip away about ¾" of insulation from the end of each wire.

4   Attach a mounting strap to the ceiling fixture box if there is not one already present. Your new light may come equipped with a strap, otherwise you can find one for purchase at any hardware store.

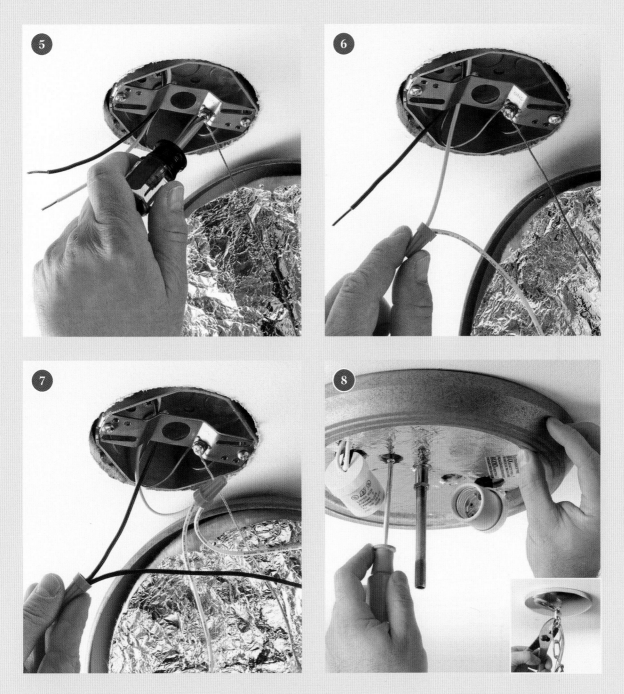

5   Lift the new fixture up to the ceiling (you may want a helper for this) and attach the bare copper ground wire from the power supply cable to the grounding screw or clip on the mounting strap. Also attach the ground wire from the fixture to the screw or clip.

6   With the fixture supported by a ladder or a helper, join the white wire lead and the white fixture wire with a wire connector (often supplied with the fixture).

7   Connect the black power supply wire to the black fixture wire with a wire connector.

8   Position the new fixture mounting plate over the box so the mounting screw holes align. Drive the screws until the fixture is secure against the ceiling. Some fixtures are supported by a threaded rod or nipple in the center that screws into a female threaded opening in the mounting strap (inset).

Recessed Ceiling Lights

Tools & Materials

Recessed-lighting can
  for new construction
  or remodeling and trim
Circuit tester
Cable ripper
Combination tool
Pliers
Fish tape
Hack saw
Drywall saw
NM cable
Work gloves
Eye protection

Recessed ceiling lights often are installed in series to provide exacting control over the amount and direction of light. Spacing the canisters in every other ceiling joist bay is a common practice.

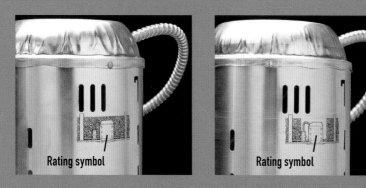

Choose the proper type of recessed light fixture for your project. There are two types of fixtures: those rated for installation within insulation (left), and those which must be kept at least 3" from insulation (right). Self-contained thermal switches shut off power if the unit gets too hot for its rating. A recessed light fixture must be installed at least ½" from combustible materials.

RECESSED LIGHTS are versatile fixtures suited for a variety of situations. Fixtures rated for outdoor use can also be installed in roof soffits and overhangs for accent and security lighting. Recessed fixtures can also be installed over showers or tubs. Be sure to use fixture cans and trims rated for bathroom use.

There are recessed lighting cans in all shapes and sizes for almost every type of ceiling or cabinet. Cans are sold for unfinished ceilings (new construction) or for finished ceilings (retrofit installation). Cans are also rated as insulation compatible or for un-insulated ceilings. Be sure to use the correct one for your ceiling to prevent creating a fire hazard.

Recessed ceiling light housings come in many sizes and styles for various purposes and budgets. Some are sold with trim kits (below) included. Some common types are: new construction recessed housing (sold in economical multipacks) (A); airtight recessed housings (for heated rooms below unheated ceilings) (B); shallow recessed housings (for rooms with 2 × 6" ceiling joists) (C); small aperture recessed housing (D); recessed slope ceiling housing (for vaulted ceilings) (E).

Trim kits for recessed ceiling lights may be sold separately. Common types include: recessed open trim (E); baffle trim (C); recessed open trim with baffle (A, F); recessed eyeball trim (B); shower light trim (D); airtight recessed trim (E).

INSTALLING RECESSED CEILING LIGHTS

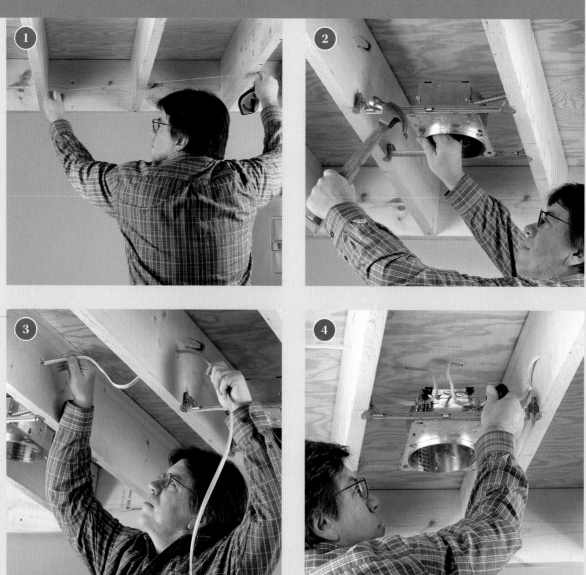

1   Mark the location for the light canister. If you are installing multiple lights, measure out from the wall at the start
    and end of the run, and connect them with a chalkline snapped parallel to the wall. If the ceiling is finished with a
    surface (wallboard), *See* next page.

2   Install the housing for the recessed fixture. Housings for new construction (or remodeling installations where the
    installation area is fully accessible from either above or below) have integral hanger bars that you attach to each
    joist in the joist bay.

3   Run electric cable from the switch to each canister location. Multiple lights are generally installed in series so
    there is no need to make pigtail connections in the individual boxes. Make sure to leave enough extra cable at each
    location to feed the wire into the housing and make the connection.

4   Run the feeder cables into the electrical boxes attached to the canister housings. You'll need to remove knockouts
    first and make sure to secure the cable with a wire staple within 8" of the entry point to the box.

5   Connect the feeder wires to the fixture wires inside the junction box. Twist the hot lead together with the black fixture wire, as well as the black lead to other fixtures further downline. Also connect the neutral white wires. Join the ground wires and pigtail them to the grounding screw or clip in the box. Finish the ceiling, as desired.

6   Attach your trim kit of choice. Normally, these are hung with torsion spring clips from notches or hooks inside the canister. This should be done after the ceiling is installed and finished for new construction projects. With certain types of trim kits, such as eyeball trim, you'll need to install the light bulb before the trim kit.

CONNECTING A RECESSED FIXTURE CAN IN A FINISHED CEILING

1   Make the hole for the can. Most fixtures will include a template for sizing the hole. Fish 14/2 cable from the switch location to the hole. Pull about 16" of cable out of the hole for making the connection.

2   Remove a knockout from the electrical box attached to the can. Thread the cable into the box; secure it with a cable clamp. Remove sheathing insulation. Connect the black fixture wire to the black circuit wire, the white fixture wire to the white circuit wire, and then connect the ground wire to the grounding screw or grounding wire attached to the box.

3   Retrofit cans secure themselves in the hole with spring-loaded clips. Install the can in the ceiling by depressing the mounting clips so the can will fit into the hole. Insert the can so that its edge is tight to the ceiling. Push the mounting clips back out so they grip the drywall and hold the fixture in place. Install the trim piece.

Hard-wired Smoke & CO Detectors

Smoke detectors and carbon monoxide (CO) detectors are required in new construction. Hard-wired carbon monoxide detectors (A) are triggered by the presence of carbon monoxide gas. Smoke detectors are available in photoelectric and ionizing models. In ionizing detectors (B), a small amount of current flows in an ionization chamber. When smoke enters the chamber, it interrupts the current, triggering the alarm. Photoelectric detectors (C) rely on a beam of light, which when interrupted by smoke triggers an alarm. Heat alarms (D) sound an alarm when they detect areas of high heat in the room.

SMOKE AND CARBON MONOXIDE (CO) alarms are an essential safety component of any living facility. All national fire protection codes require that new homes have a hard-wired smoke alarm in every sleeping room and on every level of a residence, including basements, attics, and attached garages. A smoke alarm needs to be protected with an AFCI circuit if it is installed in a bedroom.

Most authorities also recommend CO detectors on every level of the house and in every sleeping area.

Heat alarms, which detect heat instead of smoke, are often specified for locations like utility rooms,

basements, or unfinished attics, where conditions may cause nuisance tripping of smoke alarms.

Hard-wired alarms operate on your household electrical current but have battery backups in case of a power outage. On new homes, all smoke alarms must be wired in a series so that every alarm sounds regardless of the fire's location. When wiring a series of alarms, be sure to use alarms of the same brand to ensure compatibility. Always check local codes before starting the job.

Ceiling-installed alarms should be 4 inches away from the nearest wall. Smoke alarms always need to be protected with an AFCI circuit.

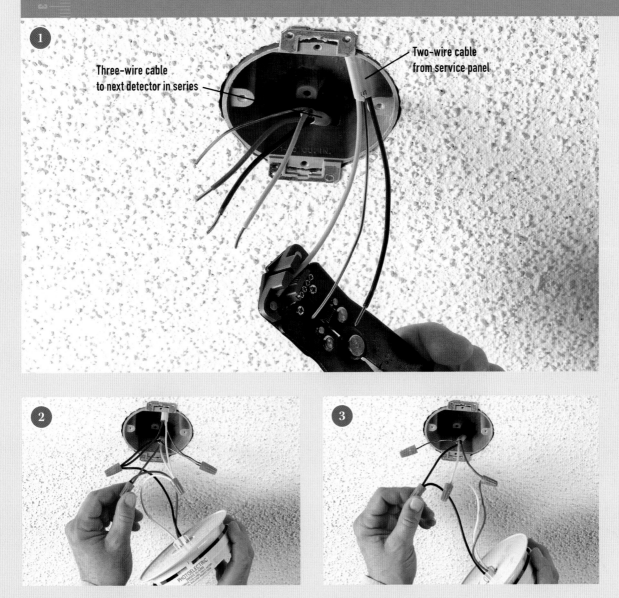

Three-wire cable to next detector in series

Two-wire cable from service panel

1   Pull 14/2 NM cable from the service panel into the first ceiling electrical box in the smoke alarm series. Pull 14/3 NM cable between the remaining alarm outlet boxes. Use cable clamps to secure the cable in each outlet box. Remove sheathing and strip insulation from wires.

2   Ensure power is off and test for power. Wire the first alarm in the series. Use a wire connector to connect the ground wires. Splice the black circuit wire with the alarm's black lead and the black wire going to the next alarm in the series. Splice the white circuit wire with the alarm's white wire and the white (neutral) wire going to the next alarm in the series. Splice the red traveler wire with the odd-colored alarm wire (in this case, also a red wire).

3   Wire the remaining alarms in the series by connecting the like-colored wires in each outlet box. Always connect the red traveler wire to the odd-colored (in this case, red) alarm wire. This red traveler wire connects all the alarms together so that when one alarm sounds, all the alarms sound. If the alarm doesn't have a grounding wire, cap the ground with a wire connector. When all alarms are wired, install and connect the new 15-amp breaker.

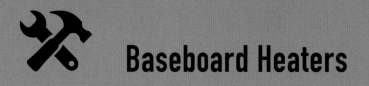

Baseboard Heaters

Tools & Materials

Drill/driver
Wire stripper
Cable ripper
Wallboard saw
Baseboard heater or heaters

240-thermostat
  (in-heater or in-wall)
12/2 NM cable
Electrical tape
Basic wiring supplies

Baseboard heaters can provide primary or supplemental heat for existing rooms or additions. Install heaters with clear space between the heater and the floor.

BASEBOARD HEATERS are a popular way to provide additional heating for an existing room or primary heat to a converted attic or basement.

Heaters are generally wired on a dedicated 240-volt circuit controlled by a thermostat. Several heaters can be wired in parallel and controlled by a single thermostat.

Baseboard heaters are generally surface-mounted without boxes, so in a remodeling situation, you only need to run cables before installing wallboard. Be sure to mark cable locations on the floor before installing drywall. Retrofit installations are also not difficult. You can remove existing baseboard and run new cable in the space behind.

Baseboard Thermostats

Single-pole thermostat   Double-pole thermostat

In-heater thermostat   Wall-mount thermostat

In-heater and wall-mount are the two types of baseboard thermostats you can choose from. If you are installing multiple heaters, a single wall-mount thermostat is more convenient. Individual in-heater thermostats give you more zone control, which can result in energy savings.

Single-pole and double-pole thermostats work in a similar manner, but double-pole models are safer. The single-pole model will open the circuit (causing shutoff) in only one leg of the power service. Double-pole models have two sets of wires to open both legs, lessening the chance that a person servicing the heater will contact a live wire.

How Much Heater Do You Need?

If you don't mind doing a little math, determining how many lineal feet of baseboard heater a room requires is not hard.

1. Measure the area of the room in square feet (length × width): _____
2. Multiply the area by 10 to get the baseline minimum wattage: _____
3. Add 5% for each newer window or 10% for each older window: _____
4. Add 10% for each exterior wall in the room: _____
5. Add 10% for each exterior door: _____
6. Add 10% if the space below is not insulated: _____
7. Add 20% if the space above is not well insulated: _____
8. Add 10% if ceiling is more than 8 ft. high: _____
9. Total of the baseline wattage plus all additions: _____
10. Divide this number by 250 (the wattage produced per foot of standard baseboard heater): _____
11. Round up to a whole number. This is the minimum number of feet of heater you need. _____

Note: It is much better to have more feet of heater than is required than fewer. Having more footage of heater does not consume more energy; it does allow the heaters to work more efficiently.

Planning Tips for Baseboard Heaters

- Baseboard heaters require a dedicated circuit. A 20-amp, 240-volt circuit of 12-gauge copper wire will power up to 16 ft. of heater.
- Do not install a heater beneath a wall receptacle. Cords hanging down from the receptacle are a fire hazard.
- Do not mount heaters directly on the floor. You should maintain at least 1" of clear space between the baseboard heater and the floor covering.
- Install heaters directly beneath windows.
- Locate wall thermostats on interior walls only, and do not install directly above a heat source.

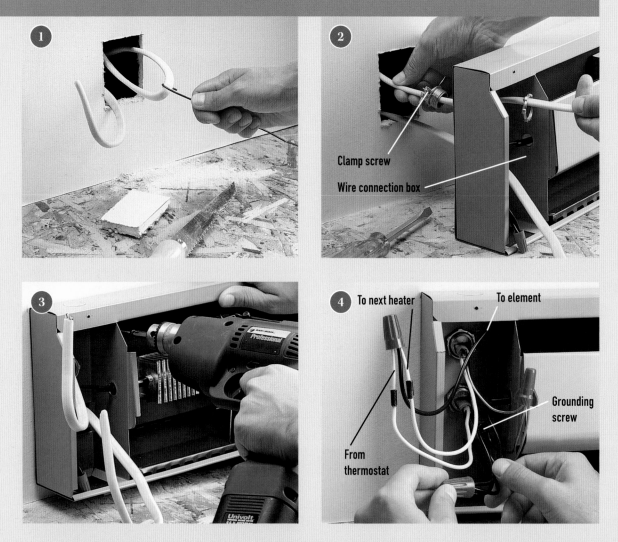

1 At the heater locations, cut a small hole in the drywall 3 to 4" above the floor. Pull 12/2 NM cables through the first hole: one from the thermostat, the other to the next heater. Pull all the cables for subsequent heaters. Middle-of-run heaters will have two cables, while end-of-run heaters have only one cable.

2 Remove the cover on the wire connection box. Open a knockout for each cable that will enter the box, then feed the cables through the cable clamps and into the wire connection box. Attach the clamps to the wire connection box, and tighten the clamp screws until the cables are gripped firmly.

3 Anchor the heater against the wall about 1" off the floor by driving flathead screws through the back of housing and into studs. Strip away cable sheathing so at least ½" of sheathing extends into the heater. Strip ¾" of insulation from each wire using a combination tool.

4 Make connections to the heating element if the power wires are coming from a thermostat or another heater controlled by a thermostat. See next page for other wiring schemes. Connect the white circuit wires to one of the wire leads on the heater. Tag white wires with black tape to indicate they are hot. Connect the black circuit wires to the other wire lead. Connect a grounding pigtail to the green grounding screw in the box, then join all grounding wires with a wire connector. Reattach cover.

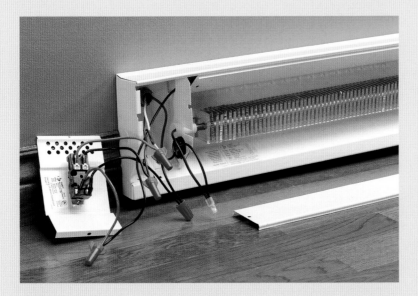

One heater with end-cap thermostat. Run both power leads (black plus tagged neutral) into the connection box at either end of the heater. If installing a single-pole thermostat, connect one power lead to one thermostat wire and connect the other thermostat wire to one of the heater leads. Connect the other hot LINE wire to the other heater lead. If you are installing a double-pole thermostat, make connections with both legs of the power supply.

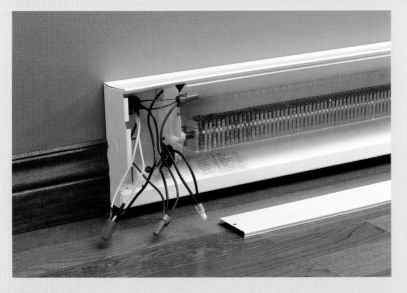

Multiple heaters. At the first heater, join both hot wires from the thermostat to the wires leading to the second heater in line. Be sure to tag all white neutrals hot. Twist copper ground wires together and pigtail them to the grounding screw in the baseboard heater junction box. This parallel wiring configuration ensures that power flow will not be interrupted to the downstream heaters if an upstream heater fails.

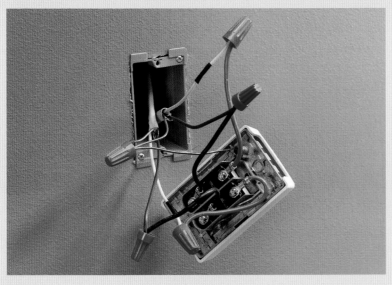

Wall-mounted thermostat. If installing a wall-mounted thermostat, the power leads should enter the thermostat first and then be wired to the individual heaters singly or in series. Hookups at the heater are made as shown in step 4. Be sure to tag the white neutral as hot in the thermostat box as well as in the heater box.

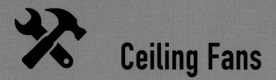

Ceiling Fans

Tools & Materials

Screwdriver
Combination tool
Pliers or adjustable wrench
Circuit tester
Hammer
Ceiling fan light kit
2 × 4 lumber or adjustable ceiling
    fan crossbrace
1½" and 3" wallboard screws
Eye protection

A ceiling fan helps keep living spaces cooler in the summer and warmer in the winter. Replacing an overhead light with a fan/light is an easy project with big payback.

CEILING FANS are installed and wired like ceiling fixtures. They always require heavy-duty bracing and electrical boxes rated for ceiling fans.

Most standard ceiling fans work with a wall switch functioning as master power for the unit. Pull chains attached to the unit control the fan and lights. In these installations, it's fairly simple to replace an existing ceiling fixture with a fan and light.

If you will be installing a new circuit for the fan, use three-wire cable so both the light and the motor can be controlled by wall switches.

Because ceiling fans generally weigh more than ceiling lights and the motion of the blade creates more stress, it is very important that the ceiling box is securely mounted and is rated for ceiling fans. Ceiling boxes rated for ceiling fans are marked with the phrase "For ceiling fan support." If your existing ceiling box is not fan-rated, replace it with one that is. And be sure to inspect the manner in which the box is mounted to make sure it is strong enough.

Installation varies from fan to fan, so be sure to follow the manufacturer's instructions.

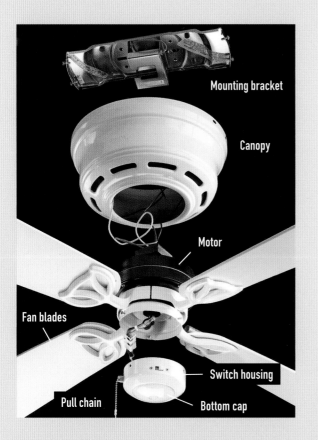

Mounting bracket

Canopy

Motor

Fan blades

Pull chain

Switch housing

Bottom cap

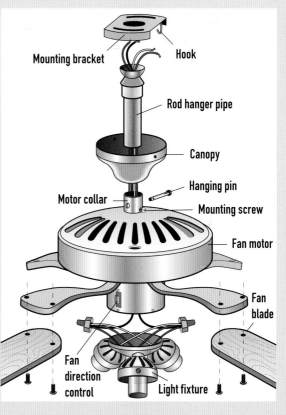

Mounting bracket — **Hook**

Rod hanger pipe

Canopy

Hanging pin

Motor collar — **Mounting screw**

Fan motor

Fan blade

Fan direction control — **Light fixture**

Bracket-mounted ceiling fans are hung directly from a mounting bracket that is attached to the ceiling box. A canopy conceals the motor and the connections.

Downrod mounted ceiling fans are supported by a metal rod that's hung from the ceiling mounting bracket. The length of the rod determines the height of the fan. Downrod fans are used in rooms with ceilings 8 ft. high or higher.

Fans that Heat

The first generation of ceiling fans did one job: they spun and moved air. As the technology advanced, light kits were added to replace the light source that is lost when a fan-only appliance is installed. Now, some ceiling fans are manufactured with electric heating elements that can produce up to 5,000 BTUs of heat, comparable to a small space heater. Located in the fan canopy, the ceramic heat elements direct heat out the vents and force it down to the living level in the room, along with the heated air that naturally rises.

Fan-mounted heaters are relatively light duty, so they generally do not require a dedicated circuit. In most cases, you can supply power to the heater/fan with any 15-amp room light circuit that has extra capacity.

Supporting Ceiling Boxes

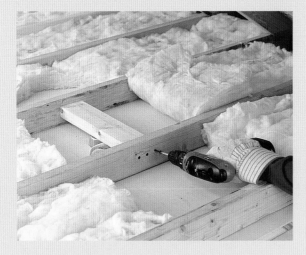

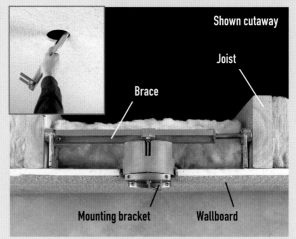

Add a wood brace above the ceiling box if you have access from above (as in an attic). Cut a 24" brace to fit and nail it between the ceiling joists. Drive a couple of deck screws through the ceiling box and into the brace. If the box is not fan-rated, replace it with one that is.

Install an adjustable fan brace if the ceiling is closed and you don't want to remove the wallcoverings. Remove the old light and the electrical box and then insert the fan brace into the box opening (inset photo). Twist the brace housing to cause it to telescope outward. The brace should be centered over the opening and at the right height so the ceiling box is flush with the ceiling surface once it is hung from the brace.

Bracket-mounted Fans

Direct-mount fan units have a motor housing with a mounting tab that fits directly into a slot on the mounting bracket. Fans with this mounting approach are secure and easy to install but difficult to adjust.

Ball-and-socket fan units have a downrod, but instead of threading into the mounting bracket, the downrod has an attached ball that fits into a hanger "socket" in the mounting bracket. This installation allows the fan to move in the socket and find its own level for quiet operation.

INSTALLING DOWNROD CEILING FANS

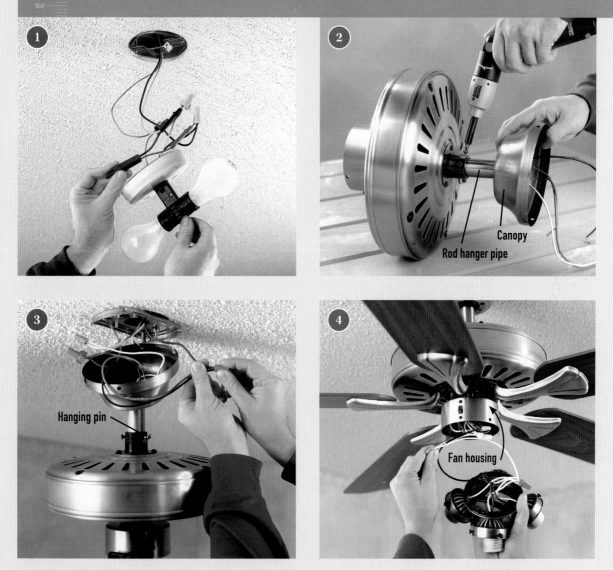

Canopy

Rod hanger pipe

Hanging pin

Fan housing

1   Shut off the power to the circuit at the service panel. Unscrew the existing fixture and carefully pull it away from the ceiling. Test for power by inserting the probes of a tester into the wire connectors on the black and the white wires. Disconnect and remove the old fixture.

2   Run the wires from the top of the fan motor through the canopy and then through the rod hanger pipe. Slide the rod hanger pipe through the canopy and attach the pipe to the motor collar using the included hanging pin. Tighten the mounting screws firmly.

3   Hang the motor assembly by the hook on the mounting bracket. Connect the wires according to manufacturer's directions using wire connectors to join the fixture wires to the circuit wires in the box. Gather the wires together and tuck them inside the fan canopy. Lift the canopy and attach it to the mounting bracket.

4   Attach the fan blades with the included hardware. Connect the wiring for the fan's light fixture according to the manufacturer's directions. Tuck all wires into the switch housing and attach the fixture. Install light bulbs. Restore power and test the fan.

Repairing Light Fixtures

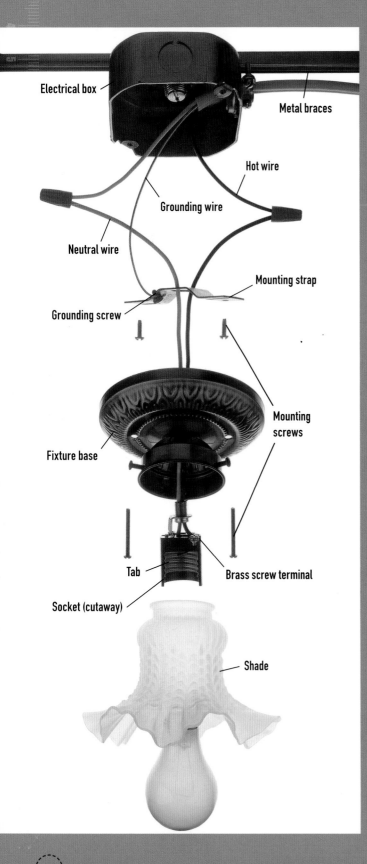

Electrical box

Metal braces

Hot wire

Grounding wire

Neutral wire

Mounting strap

Grounding screw

Mounting screws

Fixture base

Tab

Brass screw terminal

Socket (cutaway)

Shade

Tools & Materials

Circuit tester
Screwdriver
Continuity tester
Combination tool
Replacement parts, as needed

In a typical incandescent light fixture, a black hot wire is connected to a brass screw terminal on the socket. Power flows to a small tab at the bottom of the metal socket and through a metal filament inside the bulb. The power heats the filament and causes it to glow. The current then flows through the threaded portion of the socket and through the white neutral wire back to the main service panel.

LIGHT FIXTURES are attached permanently to ceilings or walls. They include wall-hung sconces, ceiling-hung globe fixtures, recessed light fixtures, and chandeliers. Most light fixtures are easy to repair using basic tools and inexpensive parts.

If a light fixture fails, always make sure the light bulb is screwed in tightly and is not burned out. A faulty light bulb is the most common cause of light fixture failure. If the light fixture is controlled by a wall switch, also check the switch as a possible source of problems.

Light fixtures can fail because the sockets or built-in switches wear out. Some fixtures have sockets and switches that can be removed for minor repairs. These parts are held to the base of the fixture with mounting screws or clips. Other fixtures have sockets and switches that are joined permanently to the base. If this type of fixture fails, purchase and install a new light fixture.

Damage to light fixtures often occurs because homeowners install light bulbs with wattage ratings that are too high. Prevent overheating and light fixture failures by using only light bulbs that match the wattage ratings printed on the fixtures.

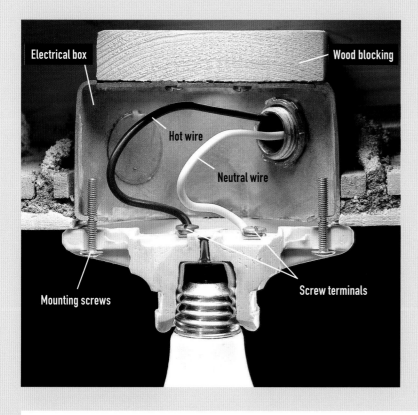

Electrical box

Wood blocking

Hot wire

Neutral wire

Mounting screws

Screw terminals

A non-compliant fixture.
Before 1959, incandescent light fixtures (shown cutaway) often were mounted directly to an electrical box or to plaster lath. Electrical codes now require that fixtures be attached to mounting straps that are anchored to the electrical boxes. If you have a light fixture attached to plaster lath, install an approved electrical box with a mounting strap to support the fixture.

Troubleshooting Fixture Problems

Problem	Repair
Wall– or ceiling–mounted fixture flickers or does not light.	1. Check for faulty light bulb. 2. Check wall switch and repair or replace, if needed. 3. Check for loose wire connections in electrical box. 4. Test socket and replace, if needed. 5. Replace light fixture.
Built–in switch on fixture does not work.	1. Check for faulty light bulb. 2. Check for loose wire connections on switch. 3. Replace switch. 4. Replace light fixture.
Chandelier flickers or does not light.	1. Check for faulty light bulb. 2. Check wall switch and repair or replace, if needed. 3. Check for loose wire connections in electrical box. 4. Test sockets and fixture wires, and replace, if needed.
Recessed fixture flickers or does not light.	1. Check for faulty light bulb. 2. Check wall switch and repair or replace, if needed. 3. Check for loose wire connections in electrical box. 4. Test fixture and replace, if needed.

Grounding screw

1   Turn off the power to the light fixture at the main service panel. Remove the light bulb and any shade or globe, then remove the mounting screws holding the fixture base to the electrical box or mounting strap. Carefully pull the fixture base away from the box.

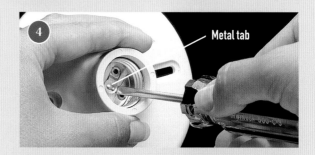

2   Test for power by touching one probe of a circuit tester to the green grounding screw, then insert the other probe into each wire connector. The tester should not glow. If it does, there is still power entering the box. Return to the service panel and turn off power to the correct circuit.

Metal tab

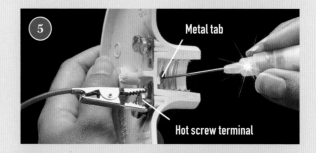

3   Disconnect the light fixture base by loosening the screw terminals. If the fixture has wire leads instead of screw terminals, remove the light fixture base by unscrewing the wire connectors.

4   Adjust the metal tab at the bottom of the fixture socket by prying it up slightly with a small screwdriver. This adjustment will improve the contact between the socket and the light bulb.

Metal tab

Hot screw terminal

5   Test the socket (shown cutaway) by attaching the clip of a continuity tester to the hot screw terminal (or black wire lead) and touching the probe of the tester to the metal tab in the bottom of the socket. The tester should glow. If not, the socket is faulty and must be replaced.

6   Attach the tester clip to the neutral screw terminal (or white wire lead), and touch the probe to the threaded portion of the socket. The tester should glow. If not, the socket is faulty and must be replaced. If the socket is permanently attached, replace the fixture.

Neutral screw terminal

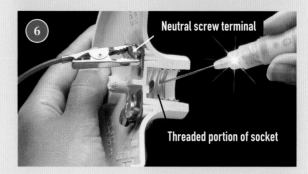

Threaded portion of socket

REPLACING A SOCKET

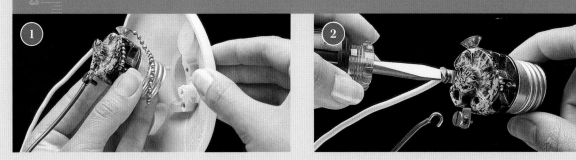

1   Remove the old light fixture. Remove the socket from the fixture. The socket may be held by a screw, clip, or retaining ring. Disconnect wires attached to the socket.

2   Purchase an identical replacement socket. Connect the white wire to the silver screw terminal on the socket, and connect the black wire to the brass screw terminal. Attach the socket to the fixture base, and reinstall the fixture.

TESTING & REPLACING A BUILT-IN LIGHT SWITCH

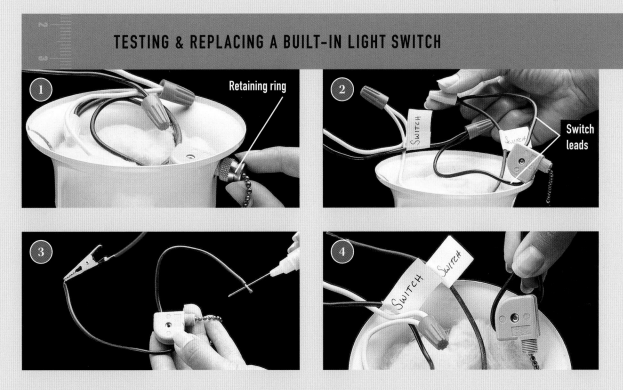

1   Remove the light fixture. Unscrew the retaining ring holding the switch.

2   Label the wires connected to the switch leads. Disconnect the switch leads and remove the switch.

3   Test the switch by attaching the clip of the continuity tester to one of the switch leads and holding the tester probe to the other lead. Operate the switch control. If the switch is good, the tester will glow when the switch is in one position, but not both.

4   If the switch is faulty, purchase and install an exact duplicate switch. Remount the light fixture, and turn on the power at the main service panel.

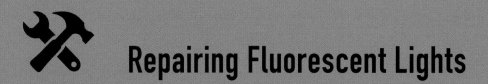

Repairing Fluorescent Lights

Tools & Materials

Screwdriver
Ratchet wrench
Combination tool
Circuit tester
Replacement tubes
Ballast (if needed)
Replacement fluorescent light fixture (if needed)

FLUORESCENT LIGHTS are relatively trouble free and use less energy than incandescent lights. A typical fluorescent tube lasts about three years and produces two to four times as much light per watt as a standard incandescent light bulb.

The most frequent problem with a fluorescent light fixture is a worn-out tube. If a fluorescent light fixture begins to flicker or does not light fully, remove and examine the tube. If the tube has bent or broken pins or black discoloration near the ends, replace it. Light gray discoloration is normal in working fluorescent tubes. When replacing an old tube, read the wattage rating printed on the glass surface, and buy a new tube with a matching rating. (*See* information below on new standards for fluorescent bulbs.) Never dispose of old tubes by breaking them. Fluorescent tubes contain a small amount of hazardous mercury. Check with your local environmental control agency or health department for disposal guidelines.

Fluorescent light fixtures also can malfunction if the sockets are cracked or worn. Inexpensive replacement sockets are available at any hardware store and can be installed in a few minutes.

If a fixture does not work even after the tube and sockets have been serviced, the ballast probably is defective. Faulty ballasts may leak a black, oily substance and can cause a fluorescent light fixture to make a loud humming sound. Although ballasts can be replaced, always check prices before buying a new ballast. It may be cheaper to purchase and install a new fluorescent fixture rather than to replace the ballast in an old fluorescent light fixture.

New Fluorescent Standards

New efficiency standards for fluorescent fixtures have recently been enacted. The old four-foot fluorescent tubes, sometimes called "fat fours" are no longer available for general use. Those tubes were called T12s, because the tube diameter was $\frac{12}{8}$ of an inch, or 1½ inches. The new tubes are called T8s and are 1 inch in diameter. The T8s use the same sockets, but do not illuminate in an old fixture because they require different ballasts. The new ballasts are electronic, as opposed to the old that were electromagnetic. A big plus of the new electronic ballasts is that they cycle much faster than the old ones. This eliminates the flicker of fluorescents that can be so annoying to some people. Another plus is that the new fixtures and bulbs produce brighter, better quality light using less power.

When your current fluorescent bulbs begin to burn out, you will need to either retrofit your fixtures with new ballasts, or purchase new fixtures. The new bulbs, ballasts, and fixtures may be slightly more expensive, but the lifespan and operating costs will be less than the older units. Simply replacing the whole fixture will require less time wiring than removing and re-wiring ballasts and sockets. If you do decide to do a re-wire, it may be easier to remove the fixture and perform the tasks on a tabletop, rather than over your head.

Tip

Recent changes to efficiency regulations mean older fluorescent tubes will soon cost more. As tubes burn out, it will make more sense to replace old fixtures with the more efficient new fixtures. The new tubes are not compatible with old fixtures.

Another advantage of the electronic ballast is that they are more sophisticated in the way they illuminate the bulb. Previous ballasts were labeled as rapid start or instant start, but now, with electronic ballasts, a programmable option is available. This technicality is probably only important in commercial settings, which use thousands of fluorescent fixtures. If you purchase separate ballasts and sockets for a retrofit, you do need to match the socket to the ballast as well as to the wattage bulb used.

Tip
Flourescent bulbs and ballasts are both hazardous waste. Check with your local waste agency for disposal locations.

Older fluorescent lights may have a small cylindrical device, called a starter, located near one of the sockets. When a tube begins to flicker, replace the entire fixture with an updated one.

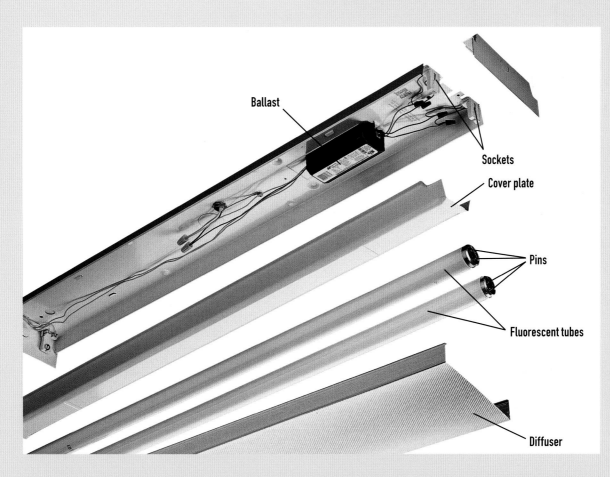

Ballast

Sockets

Cover plate

Pins

Fluorescent tubes

Diffuser

A fluorescent light works by directing electrical current through a special gas-filled tube that glows when energized. A white translucent diffuser protects the fluorescent tube and softens the light. A cover plate protects a special transformer, called a ballast. The ballast regulates the flow of 120-volt household current to the sockets. The sockets transfer power to metal pins that extend into the tube.

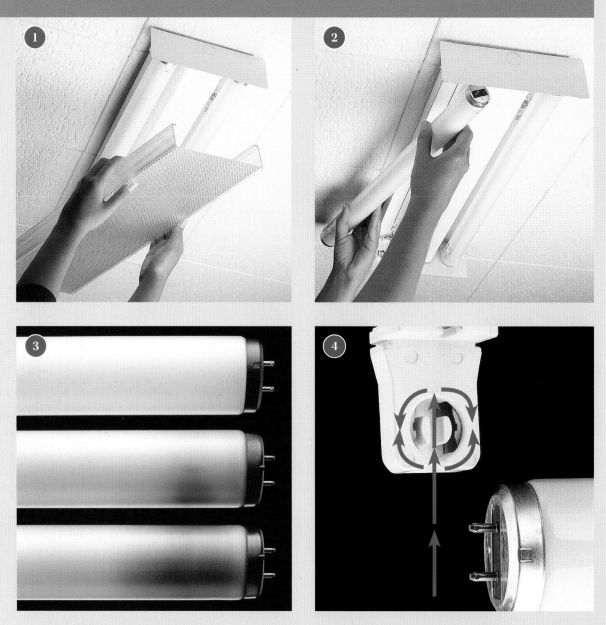

1   Turn off power to the light fixture at the switch. Remove the diffuser to expose the fluorescent tube.

2   Remove the fluorescent tube by rotating it ¼ turn in either direction and sliding the tube out of the sockets. Inspect the pins at the end of the tube. Tubes with bent or broken pins should be replaced.

3   Inspect the ends of the fluorescent tube for discoloration. A new tube in good working order (top) shows no discoloration. Normal, working tube (middle) may have gray color. A worn-out tube (bottom) shows black discoloration.

4   Install a new tube with the same wattage rating as the old tube. Insert the tube so that pins slide fully into sockets, then twist the tube ¼ turn in either direction until it is locked securely. Reattach the diffuser, and turn on the power at the main service panel.

REPLACING A SOCKET

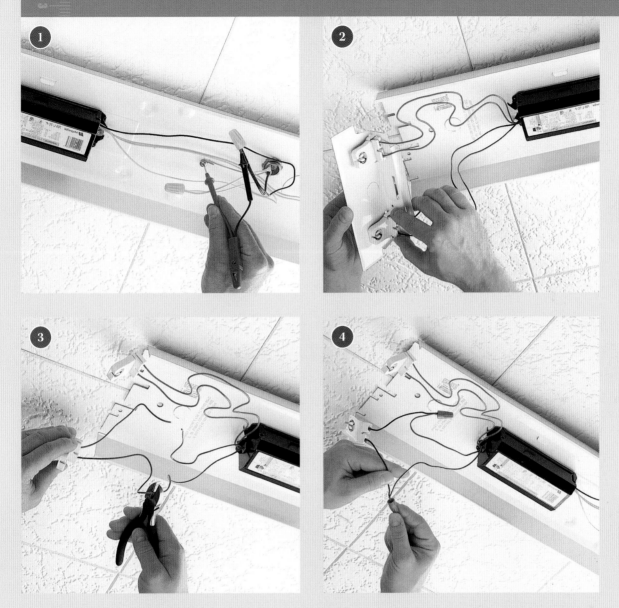

1   Turn off the power at the main service panel. Remove the diffuser, fluorescent tube, and the cover plate. Test for power by touching one probe of a neon circuit tester to the grounding screw and inserting the other probe into the hot wire connector. If the tester glows, return to the service panel and turn off the correct circuit.

2   Remove the faulty socket from the fixture housing. Some sockets slide out, while others must be unscrewed.

3   Disconnect wires attached to the socket. For push-in fittings (above) remove the wires by inserting a small screwdriver into the release openings. Some sockets have screw terminal connections, while others have preattached wires that must be cut before the socket can be removed.

4   Purchase and install a new socket. If the socket has preattached wire leads, connect the leads to the ballast wires using wire connectors. Replace the cover plate, and then the fluorescent tube, making sure that it seats properly. Replace the diffuser. Restore power to the fixture at the main service panel and test.

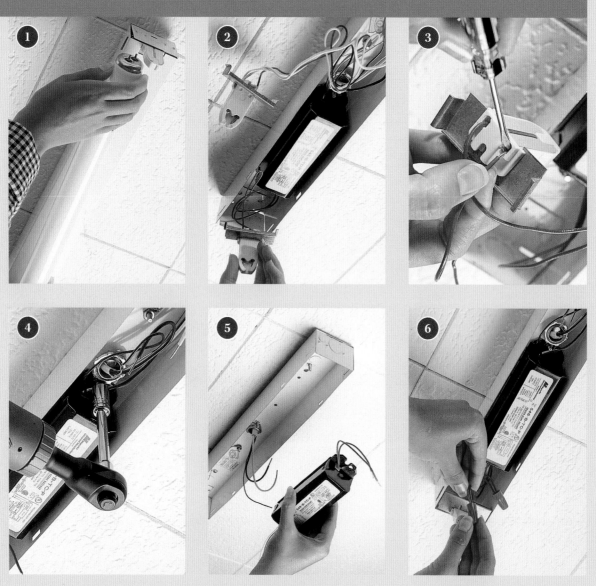

1   Turn off the power at the main service panel, then remove the diffuser, fluorescent tube, and cover plate. Test for power using a circuit tester.

2   Remove the sockets from the fixture housing by sliding them out, or by removing the mounting screws and lifting the sockets out.

3   Disconnect the wires attached to the sockets by pushing a small screwdriver into the release openings (above), by loosening the screw terminals, or by cutting wires to within 2" of sockets.

4   Remove the old ballast using a ratchet wrench or screwdriver. Make sure to support the ballast so it does not fall.

5   Install a new ballast that has the same ratings as the old ballast.

6   Attach the ballast wires to the socket wires using wire connectors, screw terminal connections, or push-in fittings. Reinstall the cover plate, fluorescent tube, and diffuser. Turn on power to the light fixture at the main service panel.

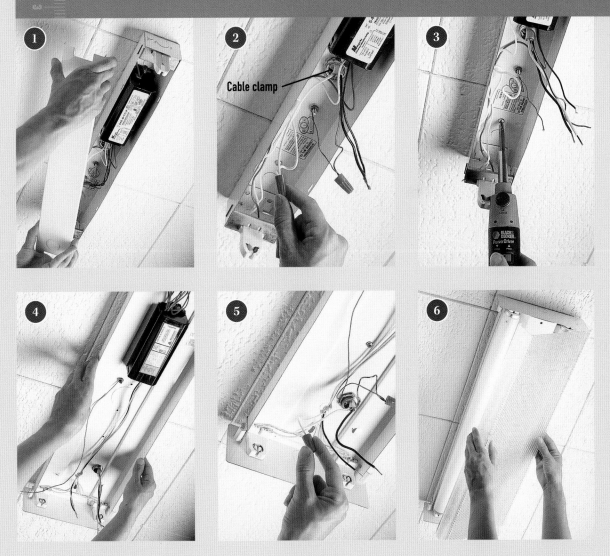

Cable clamp

1   Turn off power to the light fixture at the main service panel. Remove the diffuser, tube, and cover plate. Test for power using a circuit tester.

2   Disconnect the insulated circuit wires and the bare copper grounding wire from the light fixture. Loosen the cable clamp holding the circuit wires.

3   Unscrew the fixture from the wall or ceiling and carefully remove it. Make sure to support the fixture so it does not fall.

4   Position the new fixture, threading the circuit wires through the knockout opening in the back of the fixture. Screw the fixture in place so it is firmly anchored to framing members.

5   Connect the circuit wires to the fixture wires using wire connectors. Follow the wiring diagram included with the new fixture. Tighten the cable clamp holding the circuit wires.

6   Attach the fixture cover plate, then install the fluorescent tubes and attach the diffuser. Turn on power to the fixture at the main service panel and test.

BY MATERIAL
Service Panel
- Maintain a minimum 30" wide by 36" deep of clearance in front of the service panel.
- Ground all 120-volt and 240-volt circuits.
- Match the amperage rating of the circuit when replacing fuses.
- Use handle-tie breakers for 240-volt loads (line to line).
- Close all unused service panel openings.
- Label each fuse and breaker clearly on the panel.

Electrical Boxes
- Use boxes that are large enough to accommodate the number of wires entering the box.
- Locate all receptacle boxes 12 to 18" above the finished floor (standard).
- Locate all switch boxes 48" above the finished floor (standard). For special circumstances, inspectors will allow switch and location measurements to be altered, such as a switch at 36" above the floor in a child's bedroom or receptacles at 24" above the floor to make them more accessible for someone using a wheelchair.
- Install all boxes so they remain accessible.
- Leave no gaps greater than ⅛" between wallboard and front of electrical boxes.
- Place receptacle boxes flush with combustible surfaces.
- Leave a minimum of 6" of usable cable or wire extending past the front of the electrical box.

Wires & Cables
- Use wires that are large enough for the amperage rating of the circuit (*See* Wire Size Chart, page 28).
- Drill holes at least 2" back from the exposed edge of joists to run cables through. Do not attach cables to the bottom edge of joists.
- Do not run cables diagonally between framing members.
- Run cable between receptacles 20" above the floor.
- Use nail plates to protect cable that is run through holes drilled or cut into studs less than 1¼" from front edge of stud.
- Do not crimp cables sharply.
- Contain spliced wires or connections entirely in a plastic or metal electrical box.
- Use wire connectors to join wires.
- Use staples to fasten cables within 8" of an electrical box and every 48" along its run.

- Leave a minimum ¼" (maximum 1") of sheathing where cables enter an electrical box.
- Clamp cables and wires to electrical boxes with approved NM clamp. No clamp is necessary for one-gang plastic boxes if cables are stapled within 8".
- Label all cables and wires at each electrical box to show which circuits they serve for the rough-in inspection.
- Connect only a single wire to a single screw terminal. Use pigtails to join more than one wire to a screw terminal.

Switches
- Use a switch-controlled receptacle in rooms without a built-in light fixture operated by a wall switch.
- Use three-way switches at the top and bottom on stairways with six steps or more.
- Use switches with grounding screw with plastic electrical boxes.
- Locate all wall switches within easy reach of the room entrance.

Receptacles
- Match the amp rating of a receptacle with the size of the circuit.
- Install receptacles on all walls 24" wide or greater.
- Install receptacles so a 6-ft. cord can be plugged in from any point along a wall or every 12 ft. along a wall.
- Include receptacles in any hallway that is 10 ft. long or more.
- Use three-prong, grounded receptacles for all 15- or 20-amp, 120-volt branch circuits.
- Include a switch-controlled receptacle in rooms without a built-in light fixture operated by a wall switch.
- Install GFCI-protected receptacles in bathrooms, kitchens, garages, crawl spaces, unfinished basements, and outdoor receptacle locations.
- Install an isolated-ground circuit to protect sensitive equipment, like a computer, against tiny power fluctuations. Computers should also be protected by a standard surge protector.

Light Fixtures
- Use mounting straps that are anchored to the electrical boxes to mount ceiling fixtures.
- Keep non-IC-rated recessed light fixtures 3" from insulation and ½" from combustibles.
- Include at least one switch-operated lighting fixture in every room.

Grounding

- Ground all receptacles by connecting receptacle grounding screws to the circuit grounding wires.
- Use switches with grounding screws whenever possible. Always ground switches installed in plastic electrical boxes and all switches in kitchens, bathrooms, and basements.

BY ROOM
Kitchens/Dining Rooms

- Install a dedicated 40- or 50-amp, 120/240-volt circuit for a range (or two circuits for separate oven and countertop units).
- Install two 20-amp small appliance circuits.
- Install dedicated 15-amp, 120-volt circuits for dishwashers and food disposals (required by many local codes).
- Use GFCI receptacles for all accessible countertop receptacles; receptacles behind fixed appliances do not need to be GFCIs.
- Position receptacles for appliances that will be installed within cabinets, such as microwaves or food disposals, according to the manufacturer's instructions.
- Include receptacles on all counters wider than 12".
- Space receptacles a maximum of 48" apart above countertops and closer together in areas where many appliances will be used.
- Locate receptacles 4" above the top of the backsplash. If backsplash is more than the standard 4" or the bottom of cabinet is less than 18" from countertop, center the box in space between countertop and bottom of wall cabinet.
- Mount one receptacle within 12" of the countertop on islands and peninsulas that are 12 × 24" or greater.
- Do not put lights on small appliance circuits.
- Install additional lighting in work areas at a sink or range for convenience and safety.

Bathrooms

- Install a separate 20-amp circuit.
- Ground switches in bathrooms.
- Use GFCI-protected receptacles.
- Install at least one ceiling-mounted light fixture.
- Place blower heaters in bathrooms well away from the sink and tub.

Utility/Laundry Rooms

- Install a separate 20-amp circuit for a washing machine.
- Install a minimum feed 30-amp #10 THHN wire for the dryer powered by a separate 120/240-volt major appliance circuit.

- Install metal conduit for cable runs in unfinished rooms.
- Use GFCI-protected receptacles.

Living, Entertainment, Bedrooms

- Install a minimum of two 15-amp circuits in living rooms.
- Install a minimum of one 15- or 20-amp basic lighting/receptacle circuit for each 600 sq. ft. of living space.
- Install a dedicated circuit for each permanent appliance, like an air conditioner, computer, or group of electric baseboard heaters.
- Do not use standard electrical boxes to support ceiling fans.
- Include receptacles on walls 24" wide or more.
- Space receptacles on basic lighting/receptacle circuits a maximum of 12 ft. apart. For convenience you can space them as close as 6 ft.
- Position permanent light fixtures in the center of the room's ceiling.
- Install permanently wired smoke alarms in room additions that include sleeping areas and hallways.

Outdoors

- Check for underground utilities before digging.
- Use UF cable for outdoor wiring needs.
- Run cable in schedule 80 PVC plastic, as required by local code.
- Most local codes now require in-use rated weatherproof box covers.
- Bury cables housed in conduit at least 18" deep; cable not in conduit must be buried at least 24" deep.
- Use weatherproof electrical boxes with watertight covers.
- Use GFCI-protected receptacles.
- Install receptacles a minimum of 12" above ground level.
- Anchor freestanding receptacles not attached to a structure by embedding the schedule 80 PVC plastic conduit in a concrete footing, so that it is at least 12" but no more than 18" above ground level.
- Plan on installing a 20-amp, 120-volt circuit if the circuit contains more than one light fixture rated for 300 watts, or more than four receptacles.

Stairs/Hallways

- Use three-way switches at the top and bottom on stairways with six steps or more.
- Include receptacles in any hallway that is 10 ft. long or more.
- Position stairway lights so each step is illuminated.

Metric Conversions

Metric Equivalent

Inches (in.)	1/64	1/32	1/25	1/16	1/8	1/4	3/8	2/5	1/2	5/8	3/4	7/8	1	2	3	4	5	6	7	8	9	10	11	12	36	39.4
Feet (ft.)																								1	3	3 1/12
Yards (yd.)																									1	1 1/12
Millimeters (mm)	0.40	0.79	1	1.59	3.18	6.35	9.53	10	12.7	15.9	19.1	22.2	25.4	50.8	76.2	101.6	127	152	178	203	229	254	279	305	914	1,000
Centimeters (cm)							0.95	1	1.27	1.59	1.91	2.22	2.54	5.08	7.62	10.16	12.7	15.2	17.8	20.3	22.9	25.4	27.9	30.5	91.4	100
Meters (m)																								.30	.91	1.00

Converting Measurements

To Convert:	To:	Multiply by:
Inches	Millimeters	25.4
Inches	Centimeters	2.54
Feet	Meters	0.305
Yards	Meters	0.914
Miles	Kilometers	1.609
Square inches	Square centimeters	6.45
Square feet	Square meters	0.093
Square yards	Square meters	0.836
Cubic inches	Cubic centimeters	16.4
Cubic feet	Cubic meters	0.0283
Cubic yards	Cubic meters	0.765
Pints (U.S.)	Liters	0.473 (Imp. 0.568)
Quarts (U.S.)	Liters	0.946 (Imp. 1.136)
Gallons (U.S.)	Liters	3.785 (Imp. 4.546)
Ounces	Grams	28.4
Pounds	Kilograms	0.454
Tons	Metric tons	0.907

To Convert:	To:	Multiply by:
Millimeters	Inches	0.039
Centimeters	Inches	0.394
Meters	Feet	3.28
Meters	Yards	1.09
Kilometers	Miles	0.621
Square centimeters	Square inches	0.155
Square meters	Square feet	10.8
Square meters	Square yards	1.2
Cubic centimeters	Cubic inches	0.061
Cubic meters	Cubic feet	35.3
Cubic meters	Cubic yards	1.31
Liters	Pints (U.S.)	2.114 (Imp. 1.76)
Liters	Quarts (U.S.)	1.057 (Imp. 0.88)
Liters	Gallons (U.S.)	0.264 (Imp. 0.22)
Grams	Ounces	0.035
Kilograms	Pounds	2.2
Metric tons	Tons	1.1

Converting Temperatures

Convert degrees Fahrenheit (F) to degrees Celsius (C) by following this simple formula: Subtract 32 from the Fahrenheit temperature reading. Then mulitply that number by 5/9. For example, 77°F - 32 = 45. 45 × 5/9 = 25°C.

To convert degrees Celsius to degrees Fahrenheit, multiply the Celsius temperature reading by 9/5, then add 32. For example, 25°C × 9/5 = 45. 45 + 32 = 77°F.

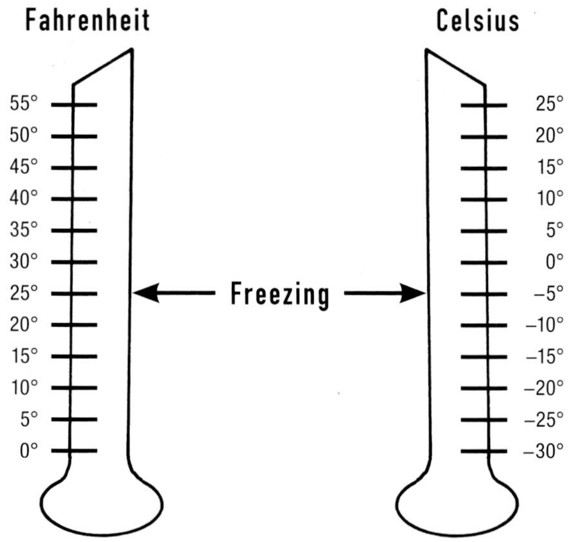

Index

First published in 2013 by Cool Springs Press, an imprint of the Quayside Publishing Group,
400 First Avenue North, Suite 400, Minneapolis, MN 55401

Cool Springs Press titles are also available at discounts in bulk quantity for industrial or sales-promotional use. For details write to Special Sales Manager at Cool Springs Press, 400 First Avenue North, Suite 400, Minneapolis, MN 55401 USA. To find out more about our books, visit us online at www.coolspringspress.com.

Library of Congress Cataloging-in-Publication Data

Homeskills. Wiring : fix your own lights, switches, receptacles, boxes, cables & more.
    pages cm
  ISBN 978-1-59186-584-1 (softcover)
  1. Electric wiring, Interior--Amateurs' manuals. I. Cool Springs Press. II. Title: Wiring. III. Title: Home skills.

TK3285.H67 2013
621.319'24--dc23

2013005620

Design Manager: Cindy Samargia Laun
Design and layout: Danielle Smith
Cover and series design: Carol Holtz

Printed in China
10 9 8 7 6 5 4 3 2 1

NOTICE TO READERS

For safety, use caution, care, and good judgment when following the procedures described in this book. The publisher cannot assume responsibility for any damage to property or injury to persons as a result of misuse of the information provided.

The techniques shown in this book are general techniques for various applications. In some instances, additional techniques not shown in this book may be required. Always follow manufacturers' instructions included with products, since deviating from the directions may void warranties. The projects in this book vary widely as to skill levels required: some may not be appropriate for all do-it-yourselfers, and some may require professional help.

Consult your local building department for information on building permits, codes, and other laws as they apply to your project.